DATE DUE

SEP 1 6 2009			
May 18, 10			

Demco, Inc. 38-293

Sustaining and Improving Learning Communities

Sustaining and Improving Learning Communities

Jodi Levine Laufgraben
Nancy S. Shapiro

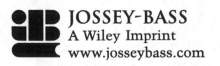

JOSSEY-BASS
A Wiley Imprint
www.josseybass.com

Published by Jossey-Bass
A Wiley Imprint
989 Market Street, San Francisco, CA 94103-1741   www.josseybass.com

Jossey-Bass books and products are available through most bookstores. To contact Jossey-Bass directly call our Customer Care Department within the U.S. at 800-956-7739, outside the U.S. at 317-572-3986 or fax 317-572-4002.

Jossey-Bass also publishes its books in a variety of electronic formats. Some content that appears in print may not be available in electronic books.

Library of Congress Cataloging-in-Publication Data

Laufgraben, Jodi Levine, 1966-
  Sustaining and improving learning communities / Jodi Levine Laufgraben, Nancy S. Shapiro.– 1st ed.
     p. cm.
  Includes bibliographical references (p.   ) and index.
  ISBN 0-7879-6054-3 (alk. paper)
  1. Universities and colleges–United States–Administration. 2. Universities and colleges–Curricula–United States. 3. Group work in education–United States. I. Shapiro, Nancy Sherman. II. Title.
  LB2341.L245 2004
  378.1'6–dc22

                                   2004006647

Printed in the United States of America
FIRST EDITION
PB Printing   10 9 8 7 6 5 4 3 2 1

THE JOSSEY-BASS

HIGHER AND ADULT EDUCATION SERIES

CONTENTS

For Ross and Morgan
—JLL

For Albert and Lucille Sherman
—NSS

And for our families, our friends, our colleagues, and our students

PREFACE

When we wrote *Creating Learning Communities* in 1999, we explored the rationale and justification for learning communities, attempting to make a case for why higher education institutions should make the investment and take the plunge into this innovative and relatively new model of reorganizing undergraduate education. We offered chapters describing the what, the how, and the why of learning communities for different types of institutions. Since then, much has happened in the higher education landscape. We have witnessed surging interest in undergraduate education reform, with learning communities commanding increased attention in the literature and on conference agendas.

The present volume addresses the sustainability and improvement of learning communities. What are the characteristics of successful, sustainable communities and what is lacking in communities that are struggling? How can institutions that began with modest programs expand and improve their initiatives?

Funding for higher education is stretched to the breaking point. Calls for accountability from internal and external forces are increasing. As a result, institutions need to explain and explore the value that learning communities add to the campus, the students, the faculty, and—more generally—the culture of higher education. Universities and colleges have to become more "intentional" about helping students succeed. Over the past decade it has become clear that college education is not just for the privileged or the wealthy, but that postsecondary education is a public good and a necessity in the complex society of the twenty-first century. National studies, such as the Association of American Colleges and Universities' (AACU) National Panel Report (2002), *Greater Expectations,* make a strong case for reforming undergraduate education in response to the new realities facing colleges and universities. Another indicator of the increased attention to the importance of student learning in undergraduate reform is the inclusion of a new set of criteria in the popular press college rankings. *U.S. News & World Reports* has added a category of promising practices in undergraduate learning, and universities and colleges are transforming themselves in new ways, such as creating learning communities to demonstrate their commitment to student learning and curricular coherence.

The original working title for this book was "Sustaining Learning Communities," a natural sequel to our first book, *Creating Learning Communities.* When we began developing plans for the second book, we drew on our experiences implementing learning communities in different settings and asked ourselves, What advice did we need as we moved beyond creating and implementing a learning communities program?

The more we began to use the term "sustain," the less comfortable we became with this notion of "sustaining," alone, to describe the improving and broadening of scope and purpose that campuses experience once they commit to developing and creating curricular learning communities. To sustain is to nourish, to keep up or prolong. To some, "sustain" might connote the idea of maintaining a steady state. Although we do advocate supporting and extending learning communities through nourishment in the forms of fiscal and human resources, professional and faculty development, and ongoing assessment, the theory and practical advice offered throughout this book go beyond providing sustenance.

Whether the goal is to expand, improve, or connect learning communities to other aspects of the student experience, success is determined by a campus's ability to understand that learning communities are not marginal to the enterprise of the institution; rather they are central to the mission. Institutions that engage in developing, sustaining, and improving learning communities are attending to the conditions under which the programs exist and operate, as well as the settings in which teaching and learning occur.

The title *Sustaining and Improving Learning Communities* conveys what campuses need to know and do to move toward achieving institutionalization of learning community programs. In this book, we have identified models and best practices that have either matured or emerged since the publication of *Creating Learning Communities.* We discuss sustaining learning communities in terms of a context for success, which includes (1) clearly defined and articulated program goals, (2) dedicated resources, (3) committed program leadership, (4) a broadening pool of participants and stakeholders, (5) credible evidence of program impact and achievement, and (6) a need for ongoing improvement and change.

Learning communities–both as programs and at the individual community level–operate within many contexts. Examining learning communities can start at the individual community level, consider the campus and neighboring community, and then extend beyond campus to the higher education landscape. Curriculum, pedagogy, faculty development, and assessment–issues at the heart of the teaching and learning mission–cut across the various contexts. This is why many of the chapter titles in this book are similar to chapter titles in *Creating Learning Communities*. We would be unfaithful to the definition and mission of curricular learning communities if we did not revisit and expand on issues, such as pedagogy and assessment, that are essential to the vitality and longevity of learning communities.

Connections to *Creating Learning Communities*

A generation of programs has moved beyond implementation into phases of sustainability, improvement, and enhancement. As an undergraduate reform model, learning communities have made the transition from an innovative "trend" to a credible and proven curricular model. Many of the learning community programs described in the first book have grown up, and with maturity come new as well as ongoing challenges.

- Are the implementation goals still relevant? Is it time for new goals?
- What are faculty and student experiences in the program? What resources do faculty members need to effectively plan and teach their communities?
- What is the current context for learning communities on campus?
- Should the program be expanded? Which new audiences or populations need to be involved?
- Is there credible evidence of program success? Will the information collected allow us to effectively improve our program?

Like any other part of the campus organization, learning community programs need to be continually reevaluated in emerging campus, community, and higher education contexts.

Organization of the Book

At the end of the first book, we used a first-person narrative style to share what we had learned. In this book, we invited more voices–colleagues and learning communities leaders–to provide lessons and examples. Chapter One offers a refresher on goals, models, and definitions, and it frames learning communities in the context of current theoretical perspectives and conditions that shape higher education. In Chapter Two, Anne Goodsell Love describes the campus culture needed to sustain learning communities. She discusses the nature of organizational change and the importance of clarifying the purpose and goals of learning communities. This chapter also provides an overview of the critical components of program success–curriculum, faculty development, assessment, and resources– topics that are discussed further in later chapters and throughout the book.

Chapters Three, Four, Five, and Six explore, in depth, the heart of curricular learning communities–teaching, learning, faculty development, and assessment. Chapter Three discusses designing and assessing the curriculum, primarily at the individual community level. This chapter also includes examples of learning communities curricula that enhance general education, deepen study in the major or preparation for professions, and promote information literacy. Chapter Four, coauthored with Daniel Tompkins, continues the discussion of curriculum with a focus on the types of pedagogy that build community. Benefits and challenges of teaching in the different models of learning communities are described. Moving from the individual community context to the program level, Chapter Five focuses on faculty development. It offers advice for planning, organizing, and assessing faculty development, along with suggestions for resources to extend faculty development beyond training meetings and workshops. Assessment is discussed throughout this book. In Chapter Six we advocate for engaging in evaluation and assessment that is purposeful and focused. Levels and tiers of evaluation are described, followed by an overview and examples of nine foci applicable to learning communities.

Chapters Seven and Eight explore two important approaches and purposes for learning communities: supporting diversity through learning communities and developing and sustaining learning communities in residence hall settings. In Chapter Seven, Emily Decker Lardner addresses diversity, a topic that is often discussed but rarely addressed in the learning communities literature. She reviews how the structure, curriculum, and pedagogy of learning communities can deepen diversity work. The experiences of several campuses are shared. Chapter Eight, contributed by David Schoem, describes the collegiate ideals embedded in the philosophy of living-learning programs and proposes a useful typology of residential educational programs. The chapter also discusses the unique challenges of residentially based learning communities and identifies specific points of sustainability based on a review of successful programs.

The book ends with suggestions for expanding our understanding of "communities of learning." Chapter Nine discusses learning communities that promote civic engagement and service learning. The shared theoretical and practical underpinnings of reform efforts in K–12 and higher education are also explored, along with examples of K–16 partnerships that broaden the communities in which our students and teachers learn.

Intended Audience

The audience for this book includes teachers and campus leaders who recognize the value of learning communities in transforming the undergraduate experience. For program developers and leaders, this book offers practical guidance for supporting teachers and assessing communities and programs. Faculty, the architects and builders of learning communities, are another important audience. Theory and advice are supported by examples drawn from the experiences of colleagues engaged in learning communities in a variety of settings: two- and four-year campuses, public and private colleges, and institutions of varied sizes and missions. As with our first book, we aimed to write *Sustaining and Improving Learning Communities* with a practical, accessible tone and content. We intentionally focused on expanding support, improving learning community programs, and sustaining change.

The reader new to learning communities can gain a basic understanding of models, definitions, and purposes, along with an in-depth overview of the elements of successful programs. Readers with emerging or established learning community programs will recognize challenges they face in broadening the scope of their programs and connecting to other aspects of the university's mission. They will also find practical advice for advancing their work.

In researching the many examples included in this book, we have expanded our own community of learning communities practitioners. We hope by sharing our experiences as well as those of our colleagues we have written a book that others can use as motivation and guidance to better understand the contexts for learning communities on their campuses.

Acknowledgments

Our own commitments to learning communities and undergraduate reform are sustained and inspired in large part because of the wonderful work of colleagues. There are many people we wish to thank for their contributions to this book. We were so fortunate that our friends and colleagues Anne Goodsell Love, Dan Tompkins, Emily Decker Lardner, and David Schoem accepted our invitation to contribute to this book. You are all valued colleagues, gifted writers, and dedicated learning communities practitioners. We are very grateful to all of our "personal communication" contacts and friends who responded to countless e-mail and phone inquiries about their programs and readily shared examples and reports. This book would not have been possible without their honesty, cooperation, and insights.

We are particularly grateful to Jean MacGregor, who is always willing to "think, pair, share," as she is a gracious and willing collaborator with whom we can brainstorm, seek advice, and share ideas. We especially thank Maryellen Weimer, Bob Midden, Barb Jacoby, Peter Ewell, Stuart Hunter, and Lou Albert for their feedback and endorsements. The reflections and advice of others helped us improve our work and writing. We are also grateful to our editor, David Brightman, who welcomed our desire to say more on learning communities and who understood how weddings, congressional campaigns, and a new baby sometimes sidetracked our progress.

Jodi Levine Laufgraben wishes to thank her colleagues at Temple University for their support and contributions to this book. A special thanks to my student assistants who helped with reference checking and research. I am again thankful to my most wonderful friend Karen Carter, who came to visit and worked her copy editing magic on early drafts of this book. To Nancy—a friend, colleague, and collaborator with whom working on this book was again a pleasure and privilege. But this time around I am most thankful for my family. Ross, you are the best, and I am grateful for your love and support. Thank you for keeping me calm and on task and for being patient with my piles, files, and clutter. To my little Morgan, my best production to date, who sat in her bouncy seat and smiled at mommy while I completed my final edits. To Bubbie and Poppy and Grandma and Pop for babysitting. It is so much easier to write with the support and love of family and friends.

Nancy Shapiro wishes to add her deep appreciation to her University System of Maryland colleagues for their support of this project. A special thanks to Gail Viamonte, my friend and colleague, and my graduate assistants, Dewayne Morgan and Jennifer Vest Frank, who offered valuable feedback and bibliographic assistance as the writing progressed. Jodi is a rock—a source of wisdom, humor, and great energy. Our collaboration is truly organic—our ideas and efforts complement each other and build exciting synergy. We are a great team! Finally, I am most grateful to my family: my parents, Albert and Lucille Sherman, whose love of learning and nurturing spirits continue to inspire me; my children, Susanna and Brian, both on a path of lifelong learning as they seek their own learning communities; and last, but certainly not least, my husband, Ira, the great love of my life.

June 2004   Jodi Levine Laufgraben
                                                              Philadelphia, Pennsylvania
                                                              Nancy S. Shapiro
                                                              College Park, Maryland

THE AUTHORS

Jodi Levine Laufgraben is the associate vice provost and director of periodic program review at Temple University. Formerly the assistant vice provost for University Studies, she has directed Temple's Learning Communities and Freshman Seminar Program since 1994 In addition to her administrative responsibilities, Jodi is an instructor in Educational Leadership and Policy Studies, teaching courses on educational administration, research design, action and collaborative research, and personnel. Nationally, Jodi is involved in several projects. She is a member of the National Advisory Board for the National Resource Center for the First-Year Experience and Students in Transition, a Fellow for the National Learning Communities Project, and was a principal investigator in the Restructuring for Urban Student Success Project. Her publications include numerous chapters and articles on learning communities and the first-year experience, the monograph *Learning Communities: New Structures, New Partnerships for Learning,* and *Creating Learning Communities* with Nancy Shapiro.

Nancy S. Shapiro is associate vice chancellor for Academic Affairs at the University System of Maryland. She was the founding director of the College Park Scholars living-learning program at the University of Maryland, which has been ranked third in the country by *U.S. News & World Reports* (2003). Currently, Shapiro serves as the statewide director of K–16 Initiatives for the University System of Maryland and is the principal investigator and project director overseeing major federal grants from the U.S. Department of Education and the National Science Foundation. Nancy has written extensively on educational reform, general education, and learning communities, including articles in *Peer Review* and *About Campus* and books, *Creating Learning Communities* (with Jodi Levine) and *Scenarios for Teaching Writing* (NCTE, 1996). Nancy serves on the Board of Trustees of Fielding Graduate Institute, the Board of Examiners of National Council for Accreditation of Teacher Education, and as a Fellow on the National Learning Communities Project. In 2004, she was awarded the Harry S. Levitan Education Prize by the Brandeis University Alumni Association.

Emily Decker Lardner currently serves as codirector of the Washington Center for Improving the Quality of Undergraduate Education, a public service center at the Evergreen State College. The Washington Center's mission is aimed at promoting access, equity, and opportunities for significant learning for all students, and the Center works primarily on starting and sustaining learning communities, campus equity and diversity projects, and math reform, particularly quantitative reasoning across the curriculum. Lardner earned her Ph.D. in American Literature at the University of Michigan (UM) and worked for ten years in the English Composition Board at UM before moving to the Washington Center. Emily is currently working on a monograph for the National Learning Community Project called "Communities of Hope: Learning Communities and Diversity."

Anne Goodsell Love is dean of the College at Wagner College and a Fellow of the National Learning Communities Project. At Wagner she is charged with merging the curricular and co-curricular programs of the college. Before coming to Wagner College, Anne was assistant dean of University College at the University of Akron. There she created, administered, and taught in learning communities designed for first-year students taking developmental courses.

David Schoem is the faculty director of the Michigan Community Scholars Program and teaches in the Sociology Department at the University of Michigan. He has served as assistant dean for Undergraduate Education and assistant vice president for Academic and Student Affairs, working on issues such as founding the Program on Intergroup Relations, Conflict, and Community; developing learning communities; establishing a diversity requirement; and implementing the First-Year Seminar Program. He is a National Learning Communities Fellow and has led faculty institutes on diversity issues through the American Association of Colleges and Universities, the Ford Foundation, and the Washington Center for Innovation in Undergraduate Education. David has written extensively on topics in higher education, including his recent article, "Transforming

Undergraduate Education: Moving Beyond Distinct Undergraduate Initiatives" (*Change Magazine*) and recent book, *Intergroup Dialogue: Deliberative Democracy in School, College, Community, and Workplace.* He is coeditor of a forthcoming book, *Engaging the Whole of Service-Learning, Diversity, and Learning Communities,* and is working on a new book, *College Knowledge: 101 Tips for the College-Bound Student.*

Daniel P. Tompkins is the director of the Intellectual Heritage Program and associate professor, Department of Greek, Hebrew, and Roman Classics at Temple University. He earned his B.A. in Classics at Dartmouth College in 1962 and his Ph.D. at Yale University in 1968. He has taught at Wesleyan University, Swarthmore College, and Dartmouth College, as well as Temple University. He helped build the Temple Department of Classics, developed the Temple Intellectual Heritage Program, and assisted in developing and supervising the Temple Core Curriculum and Learning Communities. Dan has published on a number of topics, including Thucydides, Homer, and the ancient city, as well as the poet Wallace Stevens.

Sustaining and Improving Learning Communities

CHAPTER ONE

INTRODUCTION: THE WHAT AND WHY OF LEARNING COMMUNITIES

Learning community programs have steadily increased in number as more institutions have recognized learning communities as effective structures for promoting curricular coherence, deeper learning, and community among students and teachers. The shape of higher education has also adjusted to the new realities of shifting demographics and economics. Surveys have just begun to track the pervasiveness of learning communities in higher education. A 2002 national survey of first-year academic practices conducted by the Policy Center on the First Year of College found that 62 percent of responding institutions reported "enrolling at least some cohorts of students into two or more courses" (Barefoot, 2002).

College guides now recognize that many colleges and universities have changed the way they do business in terms of the delivery of academic programs and support resources. Several now include features and rankings that identify programs, including learning communities that promote more meaningful undergraduate experiences. The *U.S. News & World Report 2003 Guide to America's Best Colleges* featured a new section on "Programs That Really Work," including a ranking of twenty-four learning communities initiatives. In a 2001 issue, *Time* honored four colleges that "know how to help newcomers survive and thrive" (McGrath, 2001, p. 3). Learning communities are described as one approach that improves first-year student persistence, and Seattle Central Community College was profiled for its extensive efforts on behalf of learning communities.

Several national survey instruments, including the National Survey of Student Engagement and the First-Year Initiative Survey, now include questions to identify students participating in learning communities so the impact of participation can be explored in depth. Results from the 2001 First-Year Initiative (FYI) Survey showed that linking first-year seminars with other academic courses reveals some advantages. In the pilot administration of the FYI instrument, 11 percent of participating campuses reported linking 80 percent or more of their first-year seminars to other courses. An additional 16 percent of survey participants linked 20 to 79 percent of their sections. When controlling for "required" (if seminar required), grading, content, and theme, sections of first-year seminars linked to learning communities had greater learning outcomes for academic skills, study skills, critical thinking, and engaging pedagogy (Swing, 2002).

What Is a Learning Community?

In *Creating Learning Communities,* we described several uses of the term "learning communities" (Shapiro and Levine, 1999). The intent was to illustrate that, within the universe of learning communities, there is a sense that no "one size fits all," and classifications, as well as models of learning communities, vary as needed to adapt to distinct campus cultures. In both *Creating Learning Communities* and this book, however, the focus is on curricular learning communities. As a common reference point, we offer the often-cited definition from the 1990 Gabelnick, MacGregor, Matthews, and Smith monograph, *Learning Communities: Creating Connections Among Students, Faculty, and Disciplines:* ". . . any one of a variety of curricular structures that link together several existing courses—or actually restructure the material entirely—so that students have opportunities for deeper understanding and integration of the material they are learning, and more interaction with one another and their teachers as fellow participants in the learning enterprise" (p. 19).

Recently, this definition has been revised to place greater emphasis on the curricular nature of learning communities and the intentional restructuring of teaching and learning experiences for students and faculty: "In higher education, curricular learning communities are classes that are linked or clustered during an academic term, often around an interdisciplinary theme, and enroll a common cohort of students. A variety of approaches are used to build these learning communities, with all intended to restructure the students' time, credit, and learning experiences to build community among students, between students and their teachers, and among faculty members and disciplines" (National Learning Communities Project website, http://learningcommons.evergreen.edu/03_start_entry.asp#1).

Learning communities initiatives share several basic characteristics. Learning communities

- Organize students and faculty into smaller groups
- Encourage integration of the curriculum
- Help students establish academic and social support networks
- Provide a setting for students to be socialized to the expectations of college
- Bring faculty together in more meaningful ways
- Focus faculty and students on learning outcomes
- Provide a setting for community-based delivery of academic support programs
- Offer a critical lens for examining the first-year experience (Shapiro and Levine, 1999, p. 3)

If you scan the websites or literature of many learning community programs, you will find mission or goal statements that include many of these characteristics. Table 1.1 includes some examples.

TABLE 1.1. GOAL AND MISSION STATEMENTS

Program	Mission or Goal Statement
Temple University www.temple.edu/lc	The Learning Communities at Temple University aim to: • Promote the integration of knowledge across disciplines • Support students' transition to college level learning • Enhance connections between and among students and teachers

TABLE 1.1. Continued

Program	Mission or Goal Statement
University of Maryland College Park Scholars http://scholars.umd.edu/	College Park Scholars is a collaborative living-learning community at the University of Maryland with the following goals: • To promote academic excellence, integrity, critical thinking, and creativity through the development of interdisciplinary knowledge, skills, and perspectives • To foster the development of a supportive and inclusive community of diverse students, faculty, and staff • To enhance the students' intellectual and personal development through service, experiential learning, and innovative curricular and co-curricular activities both on and off campus • To create an environment that enhances student development as life-long leaders, citizens, and scholars
Western Washington University http://www.wwu.edu/depts/figs/ FIGS: Freshman interest groups	The goal of the FIG is to create a learning community environment for first-year students, one that fosters their academic success and helps them connect one-on-one with faculty and peers.
St. Lawrence University http://web.stlawu.edu/fyp/history.htm FYP: First-year program	The FYP has four components, each of which can be mapped to one of the original concerns that gave birth to the program. However, the overarching goal of the FYP is the integration of the parts into a comprehensive educational experience for students and faculty alike. The FYP has become a model in contemporary higher education for its success in weaving together the strands of college life that are typically separated by departments and divisions. The fabric of the FYP is a tapestry woven of these four threads: the course, the communication skills component, the advising component, and the residential component.

Program	Mission or Goal Statement
UCLA (College of Letters and Science) http://www.college.ucla.edu/ge/clusters/	The College's General Education Cluster Program is a curricular initiative that is designed to strengthen the intellectual skills of entering freshmen, introduce them to faculty research work, and expose them to such "best practices" in teaching as seminars and interdisciplinary study.
LaGuardia Community College http://www.lagcc.cuny.edu/stuinfo/ firstyear/learningcomm.asp	LaGuardia's learning communities reflect a truly integrated practice: each is organized around a theme, and faculty meet regularly to plan, refine, and evaluate curriculum integration and student success.
Daytona Beach Community College http://www.dbcc.cc.fl.us/academics/ learningcommunity/index.htm	A Learning Community is a nurturing, supportive educational environment that is the outcome of organizing courses and related educational activities in such a way that: • Any participating group of students spends more time together than they would if they were only in a single course together. • Courses and activities are linked to one another. • Faculty and staff are sensitive and responsive to students' education needs.

Models

Learning communities can take different forms and be located in different places in the academic program. There are, however, four commonly described approaches or models for configuring learning communities: (1) paired or clustered courses, (2) cohorts in large courses or FIGs (freshman interest groups), (3) team-taught programs, and (4) residence-based learning communities, models that intentionally link the classroom-based learning community with a residential life component. The Learning Communities Directory maintained by the National Learning Communities Project in partnership with the Washington

Center for Improving the Quality of Undergraduate Education at the Evergreen State College is a useful resource for locating examples of learning community programs: http://learningcommons.evergreen.edu/.

Paired or Clustered Courses

Paired- or clustered-course learning communities link individually taught courses through cohort and often block scheduling (scheduling of courses in back-to-back time slots). The paired-course model links two courses and is considered a basic approach to learning communities in terms of curricular integration. A paired-course learning community typically enrolls a group of twenty to thirty students in two courses. Offerings tend to be existing courses that traditionally enroll significant numbers of first-year students. One of the two courses in the pairing is usually a basic composition or communications course. These courses tend to be more interdisciplinary in nature and promote a classroom environment in which students and faculty get to know each other (Levine Laufgraben, 2004; MacGregor, Smith, Matthews, and Gabelnick, 2002; Shapiro and Levine, 1999).

In paired-course learning communities, classes are often linked based on logical curricular connections and skill areas. For example, a pairing of calculus with general chemistry can promote scientific discovery and quantitative reasoning skills, whereas a pairing of Introduction to Sociology and College Writing could emphasize exploration of the self and society. Pairings might also include a section of a one- to three-credit student success or first-year experience course.

Clusters expand the paired-course model by linking three or four individually taught courses around a theme. Clusters are often small and usually enroll cohorts of twenty to thirty students. One course tends to be a writing course, and the cluster usually includes a weekly seminar. The weekly seminar plays an important role in helping students and faculty build curricular connections between the courses. These seminars are ideal settings for synthesis and community-building activities. Some cluster models include larger lecture-type courses in which the student cohort enrolls as a subset but then also enrolls in a smaller cluster-only seminar or writing class.

Cohorts in Large Courses

These learning communities are often referred to as "FIGs"–freshman interest groups. FIGs are the simplest model in terms of organization and cost (Gabelnick, MacGregor, Matthews, and Smith, 1990). This approach works well at large universities or at other institutions where freshmen are typically enrolled in at least one or two large lecture courses in which the learning communities students represent a subset of the total enrollment. When a large lecture course also requires enrollment in a smaller recitation or discussion session, FIG students are typically enrolled in a designated learning community section. In addition to one or two large courses, FIGs typically include a smaller writing course and a weekly seminar limited to FIG students. An undergraduate peer teacher typically leads the weekly seminar (Levine Laufgraben, 2004; MacGregor, Smith, Matthews, and Gabelnick, 2002; Shapiro and Levine, 1999).

A less commonly used approach is the federated learning community in which student cohorts enroll in larger courses along with a teacher who serves as master learner. The federated learning community integrates courses around a theme. The master learner facilitates a weekly seminar to help students synthesize what they are learning. The master learner usually has no teaching responsibilities beyond the federated learning community (Gabelnick, MacGregor, Matthews, and Smith, 1990).

Team-Taught Programs

Team-taught learning communities, also called coordinated studies programs, enroll varying numbers of students in two or more courses organized around an interdisciplinary theme. Team-taught programs represent the most extensive approach in terms of curricular integration and faculty involvement. Some require full-time faculty and student involvement, but participation can also be part-time, involving two to five courses. On many campuses, the learning community constitutes students' entire schedules for at least one semester and sometimes an entire academic year.

Themes are faculty-generated and interdisciplinary. Themes can be broad and liberal arts based, emphasize skill development in related disciplines, or prepare students for study or practice in professions. Small group discussion sections are an important part of the community. Students and a faculty member break off into smaller groups to build upon what is being learned in the other courses in the community or discuss assigned texts (book seminars).

Total community enrollment varies but can range from forty to seventy-five students. In larger team-taught programs, the cohort is often subdivided into smaller seminar groups to achieve a faculty-to-student ratio of one faculty member to twenty or twenty-five students (Gabelnick, MacGregor, Matthews, and Smith, 1990). Due to increasing fiscal pressures, typical enrollment in these programs are now more likely to be closer to seventy-five students and three teachers, with a teacher-student ratio of twenty-five to one (Levine Laufgraben, 2004; MacGregor, Smith, Matthews, and Gabelnick, 2002; Shapiro and Levine, 1999).

Residence-Based Programs

A fourth approach to learning communities, residence-based programs, involves the adaptation of a particular curricular model to include a residential component. (Chapter Eight discusses living-learning programs in greater detail.) A primary goal of residence-based education is the integration of students' living and academic environments. Residence-based learning communities go beyond assigning students with similar majors to the same floor of a residence hall. In residence-based learning communities, intentionally organized student cohorts enroll in specified curricular offerings and reside in dedicated living space.

Residence-based learning communities are designed to integrate diverse curricular and co-curricular experiences. For this reason, residence-based learning communities may be the most radical of the four learning communities approaches because they require change within multiple university systems: curriculum, teaching, and housing (Shapiro and Levine, 1999). The curricular component of residence-based programs typically resembles one of the three learning communities approaches described above: clusters, FIGS, or team-taught programs. Academic and co-curricular community activities are scheduled in residence halls, and in many instances classes actually meet in classrooms located in residential spaces (Levine Laufgraben, 2004; MacGregor, Smith, Matthews, and Gabelnick, 2002; Shapiro and Levine, 1999).

Why Learning Communities? Understanding Learning Communities in the Current Context of Undergraduate Education

The rational for learning communities is discussed in greater detail in *Creating Learning Communities* (Shapiro and Levine, 1999). The justification for learning communities, however, is also raised in this chapter, in the context of program improvement and sustainability, since more recent reports and research point to the ongoing need for reform in undergraduate education. Understanding the structure and purpose of learning communities helps explain why learning communities are a particularly useful curricular model for the current context of undergraduate education. For the past ten years, higher education has been coming to terms with a new reality. Funding challenges include rising tuition, skyrocketing enrollment projections, and diminishing state funding for public institutions. There is also pressure from business and industry to focus on workforce development in place of traditional liberal education values.

The past several decades have led to a growing universality for higher education, which has resulted in a rapidly changing demographic profile. More than 70 percent of all high school graduates go on to some form of postsecondary education. About one-third of all students in four-year institutions begin their college careers in community colleges, and many students enrolling in four-year programs take one or more courses at colleges other than the one from which they graduate (Adelman, 1999).

While more students aspire to attend college, research suggests that fewer and fewer are prepared to succeed. Forty percent of students in four-year institutions take remedial courses, and more than 60 percent of community college students require remedial education (Venezia, Kirst, and Antonio, 2003). The implications of these realities for students lead more institutions to consider cohort models, such as learning communities, to bridge the gap between what students bring to college and what they expect to take with them when they leave.

Because of the expanding role that higher education now plays in American society, it is both easier and harder to grasp the distinguishing features of the traditional "undergraduate" experience. On-line courses, distance education options, the growing role of community colleges, the increasing number of nontraditional-aged students, and the rising costs of college all contribute to this phenomenon. Colleges and universities see learning communities as one effective way to create greater coherence for college students.

In the current climate of K–16 school reform, public four-year colleges and universities are expected to create seamless transitions from high school to college. This requires clarifying their standards and providing support services for an entering student population that is increasingly diverse, with a higher percentage of first-generation students than ever before. According to a national survey ("The Chronicle Survey of Public Opinion on Higher Education," 2003), public opinion is still very favorable toward higher education, as compared to attitudes toward public schools. However, the public wants evidence of the value of higher education: evidence of student persistence, actual performance, what subjects students study, student engagement with effective practices, and overall effects of college on students (Edgerton, 2003).

Many national commissions that have initiated recent higher education reform studies raise questions about the quality of the undergraduate experience and the intended outcomes of the undergraduate curriculum. A number of national reports, including those funded by the Pew Charitable Trusts, the Carnegie Foundation, and the U.S. Department of Education, specifically addressed the changing nature of higher education. These reports shared some basic assumptions:

1. That higher education cannot continue to operate in a "silo" separate from the K–12 education community
2. That the current college-going population is dramatically different from the earlier, traditional-aged student population

3. That the public, which previously left higher education to provide its own quality control, now demands increased public accountability

AACU's Greater Expectations: A New Vision for Learning as a Nation Goes to College

In 2002, the Association of American Colleges and Universities (AACU) convened a national panel to assess and make recommendations about the overall outcomes of a college education, including general education. The *Greater Expectations* report took stock of the current American college-going population and the American college experience. Over a period of two years, the panel convened hearings and site visits, identified best practices, and arrived at consensus about the goals of a liberal education after identifying twenty-two exemplary institutions. The findings are predicated on new understandings about the role college education plays in contemporary American society and offer a good starting point for reevaluating undergraduate education.

The panel asked the question, "What is the learning that students need for the twenty-first century?" The response: "practical liberal education" (p. xi). The panel called for students to become "intentional learners, who can adapt to new environments, integrate knowledge from different sources, and continue learning throughout their lives" (p. xi). The report defined general education as "the part of a liberal education curriculum shared by all students at an institution, it provides broad exposure to multiple disciplines and forms the basis for developing important intellectual and civic capacities" (p. 25). This report suggested that content, without active, engaged learning, will not fulfill the "greater expectations" for higher education in the twenty-first century.

They called for higher education to create academic curricula and structures that will engage students in "deep learning," preparing them not just for the workforce but also for their place in the world. They also identified four higher-level outcomes that characterize a well-educated person:

- A solid knowledge of disciplines that explore the physical and social realms, together with a grasp of their characteristic modes of inquiry and findings
- Strong analytical, communication, and practical skills–acquired and applied through study in a range of fields and through experiential learning
- An examined framework of ethical, civic, and social responsibilities–and of their implications for democratic and global citizenship
- "Intention" and integrative capacities that support continuous learning [Schneider, 2003, pp. 15–16]

AAU: Standards for Success

The Association of American Universities (AAU) commissioned a two-year study of twenty research universities to answer one overriding question: "What must students know and be able to do in order to succeed in entry-level university courses?" The resulting report, *Standards for Success: Understanding University Success* (Conley, 2003), provides a set of articulated standards in liberal arts content areas: English, mathematics, social sciences, foreign language, science, and the arts. It is interesting that the key competencies that college faculty identified as the most critical for student success were "habits of mind that students develop in high school and bring with them to university studies." These habits of mind include critical thinking, analytic thinking, and problem solving; an inquisitive nature and interest in taking advantage of what a research university has to offer; the willingness to accept critical feedback and adjust based on such feedback; openness to possible failures; and the ability and desire to cope with frustrating and ambiguous learning tasks (p. 8).

These outcomes parallel the description of the liberal learning outcomes described in the AACU (2002) report *Greater Expectations*. They are also often articulated as the learner-centered curricular goals of learning communities. Institutions investing in learning communities or expanding current programs should be aware of this research and dialogue driving higher education reform.

Pew Forum on Undergraduate Education

From 2000 to 2003, Russ Edgerton, director of the Pew Forum on Undergraduate Education, convened a group of higher education innovators from across the country in a series of conferences sponsored by the Pew Charitable Trusts. The Pew Forum is an initiative that serves as an umbrella for the higher education grantees that Pew supported from 1997 to 2000 (http://www.pewundergradforum.org). The goal of the Pew grants to higher education in the late 1990s was to "call attention to the new twenty-first century landscape—trends such as the rising influence of the marketplace, the growing interest in what students can actually *do* with the knowledge they have acquired, the growing tendency of students to assemble courses from multiple providers, and the implications of new technologies," according to Edgerton (http://www.pewundergradforum.org/wp1.html).

Edgerton (2003) identified a number of emerging concerns facing higher education. First, *students are changing*. Their lives reflect the increasing complexity of their world. They have multiple commitments; many attend more than one institution before they graduate; they invest less in learning; they are increasingly motivated by the credentialing value of college rather than by meaningful "deep learning" associated with mature analytical thinking (Edgerton, 2003). Second, *universities and colleges are changing* as they respond to marketing pressures and new competitors. Size, scale, part-time faculties, remediation, technology—these and other trends challenge traditional academic communities to redefine themselves as well as their essential purposes and fundamental commitments. Edgerton postulates that in today's society, it is even more urgent that higher education communicates clear goals.

> America has been transformed from a country of small towns where life was whole and local to an industrial country where work is specialized to a post-industrial and truly global society. In such a society, it is harder and harder for all of us to feel connected to the expanding, larger community of which we are a part. And it is harder and harder to understand the basic decisions that control our lives or to feel that we have any control over these decisions. The challenges that complexity poses come home most dramatically when we consider the tasks and responsibilities of being a citizen in such a complex society. The average citizen now confronts an agenda of issues that have arisen from scientific/technical processes only experts truly understand. . . . One has to act on one's beliefs. Armchair citizenship isn't enough. To be effective citizens, people must feel that they can make a difference. Educating for a society of ever-spreading complexity involves educating for many different qualities. But above all, it involves educating for a *sense of responsibility* toward the larger community [Edgerton, 2003, p. 22].

Unless students grasp the difference between knowing and understanding and learn to be flexible and responsive in a complex and changing world, higher education will not fulfill its role in preparing the next generation for an uncertain future. In such an environment, learning communities become an important tool for organizing higher education institutions around individual learning and community responsibility.

Conclusion: The Current State of Learning Communities

From early reports such as *Involvement in Learning* (National Institute of Education, 1984) to more recently commissioned studies discussed here, calls for learner-centered environments that promote active and collaborative learning continue. These reports challenge colleges and universities to rethink the traditional classroom structure and implement new models of teaching and learning that engage and partner students and faculty in the academic enterprise. Many campuses are heeding this challenge and look to learning communities to fulfill the mission of enhancing learning outcomes, as well as student success and persistence. It is not surprising then that across the higher education landscape, learning communities are considered a national movement.

In a 2001 learning communities–themed issue of *Peer Review,* Barbara Leigh Smith revisited learning communities past and present and examined the challenges facing learning community programs: "The history of learning communities is an evolving story of reformers and innovators doing their work. It is a story about the power of personal commitments and relationships in building reform efforts. It is also a story about the power of institutional structures, processes and value systems shaping our institutions. There is continuity over time with a number of themes in this learning community history. The themes of democracy, access, and classrooms as community particularly stand out" (p. 7).

Smith cautioned that the success of learning communities as a movement cannot be determined solely by the ever-growing number of programs. Established and developing programs share four important challenges: (1) student learning and faculty development, (2) diversity, (3) institutional change, and (4) purpose (p. 7). Planners of and participants in learning communities must confront these challenges at the course, community, program, and institutional levels. Many campuses focus early attention on the size of their programs or the number of communities offered. The real challenges and true measures of success, however, lie with quality of the learning communities experience and the campus's ability to truly transform curriculum and teaching in meaningful and measurable ways.

"What matters in college" has not changed significantly since Astin authored the book by the same title in 1993. What has changed are the numerous studies and reports that confirm what we know about learning and good practice in undergraduate education, the number of institutions engaging in some type of curricular and structural reform to achieve more positive outcomes for students, and the growing demand for accountability and assessment that requires institutions to demonstrate they are meeting these outcomes. Learning communities create multidimensional learning environments and experiences for students and faculty grounded in what matters in college (Shapiro and Levine, 1999). Moving beyond the design and implementation phases of creating these types of learning environments requires deepening, broadening, and improving the scope and purpose of curricular learning communities on a campus.

CHAPTER TWO

A CAMPUS CULTURE FOR SUSTAINING LEARNING COMMUNITIES

Anne Goodsell Love

Much has been written about how to create learning communities, as many new programs have emerged in the past decade. The variety of programs matches the variety of institutions–from public to private, community college to comprehensive college to research university–and the populations of students involved are varied as well, from students in developmental-level courses to honors programs, from commuters to residents. Regional networks have been developed to support new learning communities; conferences are devoted to the topic. Granting agencies have supported learning communities at individual campuses, and both the Fund for the Improvement of Postsecondary Education (FIPSE) and the Pew Charitable Trusts supported the development of a national network aimed at improving the quality and degree of institutionalization of campus efforts.

There is considerable agreement about the desirability of restructuring parts of the undergraduate learning experience as learning communities. The actual accomplishment of this, however, continues to be an uphill battle that requires continual infusions of resources. Consider the image of a fifty-foot luxury cruiser being propelled through the water. To get it moving requires full throttle, but once it reaches a constant speed, the momentum helps carry it along, and so some of the forward thrust can be scaled back. In successfully getting the cruiser moving, the questions are, How much energy is needed to start it, how much is required to keep it going, and when can the throttle be scaled back while still maintaining the desired momentum? Learning communities at many campuses face similar questions of momentum, continued availability of resources, and resistance. For people involved with learning communities at those institutions, questions of sustainability are taking center stage.

In her essay, "The Challenge of Learning Communities as a Growing National Movement," Barbara Leigh Smith states: "If the learning community movement is to have lasting impact, the challenge of institutional change needs serious attention" (Smith, 2001, p. 8). She follows with a succinct list of items needing attention: "leadership structures, resource investments, faculty development, real curriculum integration, assessment, and pedagogical change" (p. 8). Indeed, the process of implementing long-lasting learning communities is no less daunting than the process of institutional reform; on some campuses it may be more like institutional revolution.

Sustainability of Learning Communities

This chapter explores organizational change. Understanding the nature of change is crucial to the success of learning communities from the design phase through implementation and especially for campuses trying to improve and sustain their programs. On the one hand, colleges and universities are conservative institutions charged in part with preserving cultural and social norms, so resistance to change can be a normal, healthy response (Shapiro and Levine, 1999). On the other hand, colleges and universities must respond to the changing needs of society, so it is incumbent on faculty and administrators to overcome resistance to change. Moreover, attention must be paid to *sustaining* change. Understanding organizational dynamics and organizational change, and their applicability to curricular reform, can help learning communities practitioners meet the challenges of sustaining learning communities. Other factors that have an impact on the sustainability of learning communities include

- Purposes for learning communities
- Integration of learning communities within the core mission of the institution
- Stability of campus leadership
- Expansion of the learning community leadership network across campus
- Continued buy-in of groups across campus in addition to faculty
- Extent of curricular integration
- Sustained faculty development
- Availability of resources
- Assessment

Examples from a variety of campuses will be used to illustrate the impact of these factors and conditions, many of which are addressed in greater detail in later chapters or as ongoing themes throughout the book.

To gain more insight into the factors that influence the sustainability of learning communities, consider the case of learning community implementation at Worst Case Scenario University. Although fictitious, elements of this case occur at many campuses that are attempting reform, whether it is building learning communities or implementing some other type of curricular innovation.

With mediocre retention rates, sagging financial resources, poor student and faculty morale, and a mission to "be all things to all people," Worst Case Scenario University has hit tough times. The provost has read and heard about the positive retention results of learning community programs around the country, so she and a team of faculty and administrators attend a regional conference where they learn the nuts and bolts of implementing learning communities. Back on their campus, they select a model that is in place at Small Liberal Arts College, since it seems the least complicated in terms of the use of faculty teams, integrated topics and assignments, and scheduling. The provost works with the vice president for student affairs, and together they ask the director of academic advising and the registrar to work out the details and register students for the program. Faculty are paired up, and a couple of weeks before the semester starts, a kickoff luncheon is held so that the faculty teams can get to know one another. At the end of the semester and at the end of the year, retention rates are compared for those students in and out of the program. Also at the end of the year, the provost steps down from her position, citing a desire to spend more time on her research. No one really notices that learning communities are not offered the following year.

This fictitious case is instructive in a number of ways. It is typical of a problem-solving approach that has been labeled "the garbage can model" (Cohen and March, 1974) because it puts the solution before the problem. The problem is broadly defined as high levels of student attrition, but there is no examination of the unique needs of the campus, curriculum, faculty, or students at Worst Case. Without a purpose beyond keeping students at the university, a learning community approach is chosen that involves minimal integration and barely scratches the structural surface of the institution. Faculty are not given the opportunity or resources for integrating their courses or for structuring the social interactions of their communities. Assessment is thought of only in terms of retention, which is reasonable, since that and an improved financial situation for the university were the only goals set. Finally, the person who had the idea of bringing learning communities to the campus is no longer in a prominent leadership position. Without broad support for the initiative across many departments, the lack of leadership from the provost results in an abandonment of the program.

Organizational Change

The learning communities at Worst Case Scenario University were implemented with little attention to the campus's commitment to or readiness for change. Curricular reform involves an understanding of the dynamics of organizational change and the ability to do more than make technical modifications to the academic system. The literature on organizational change is plentiful (Birnbaum, 1988; Daft, 2001; Jones, 2001; Peterson, Dill, Mets, and Associates, 1997; Vaill, 1996), and much of it recognizes the many difficulties inherent in any change process. A change process with the potential to reexamine the fundamental purpose of the enterprise—such as the purpose of higher education—will have substantially different challenges than a change process that tinkers around the edges, addressing perceived needs in a fragmentary manner. Colleges and universities face an "adaptive challenge" (Heifetz and Laurie, 1997) in that they are under increased public scrutiny and face increased competition for students and resources while they struggle to come to terms with new technologies. Colleges also must balance the nation's demands for a skilled workforce with the academy's belief in producing citizens who can sustain the values of a democratic community. This type of adaptive challenge differs from a purely technical challenge because it has the potential to do different things in different ways. In developing learning communities, the challenge is not to offer more sections of existing courses or new courses but to change relationships between courses, faculty, and students.

If colleges and universities are to address adaptive challenges in higher education, a first step in the change process must be to break away from structures with fixed responses and actions that do not allow for new patterns (Barczak, Smith, and Wilemon, 1987). "The disciplinary hold on curriculum, a course-and-credit system of academic bookkeeping, and the atomism of faculty reward systems all stand as formidable impediments to the educational renewal to which campuses aspire" (Schneider and Shoenberg, 1999, p. 34). A conversation that is common to early implementation stages of learning communities includes questions about "counting" team-taught courses for faculty load and student credit hours and questions about the placement of interdisciplinary courses within traditional academic departments (What course prefix does it get? Which department chair is responsible for the course?). Reshaping fixed structures into systems with more permeable membranes is difficult work. Often it represents a substantial obstacle to campuswide implementation of learning communities, let alone sustainability. Learning communities may start in one corner of a campus, but their extension across the institution may fail due to a lack of the true pattern breaking and experimentation that needs to occur on a systemic, campuswide level.

Even at colleges and universities ready for an adaptive challenge, learning communities copied and pasted from programs at other campuses without sufficient analysis of the adopting campus's unique needs and resources may face issues of sustainability because they were never the right fit. Organizations that move too quickly to a solution may temporarily relieve some of the uncomfortable feelings that result from uncertainty but fail to address or recognize all the facets of the problem (Heifetz and Laurie, 1997). Again, clarity of the purpose of a change is critical to its success, not just because it will be easier to recognize success but also because clarity of purpose drives decisions regarding program implementation.

Obstacles to Change

Lack of agreement about the need for or purpose of reform on campus and unclear decision-making structures are two of several obstacles to innovation articulated by William Tierney (2001). Neither is unique to higher education, but both tend to be characteristic of colleges and universities. Faculty autonomy is highly valued in higher education, but it results in a relatively flat organizational structure. That, coupled with the high value placed on deliberative processes (decision making by committee, with much input from many constituents), can make for unclear decision-making structures and timelines. All contribute to a scenario in which reform efforts can get bogged down in discussion, debate, and disagreement.

These two obstacles contribute to a third: that in discussing the merits of a proposed change and the methods by which the change may be made, it is easy to forget to consider how the change will be evaluated (Tierney, 2001). Fourth, although members of a committee or two may be convinced of the need for reform and immersed in details of implementation, the rest of the campus may be unaware of their work. Unless progress is measured and shared with the campus, the reform effort may never build the momentum it needs to become institutionalized. At Worst Case Scenario University, the early adopters failed to involve the greater campus community in the effort, so when the provost stepped down, motivation and momentum were lost. Finally, the fifth obstacle to change results when reformers become exhausted by the effort put forth and may be reluctant to tackle any future change.

Tierney (2001) recommends addressing these obstacles as a way to sustain reform. Specifically, he recommends that committee members be selected and primed with an eye toward effective action so they are clear about their charge. "The next step is to lay out the process for reaching a decision. What roles will committee members play? Who will be responsible for what issue? Similarly, specific time frames must be outlined so that members can decide how often the committee should meet and what needs to be done by a certain date" (Tierney, 2001, p. 23). Other key actions involve developing benchmarks for measurement and communicating information with the rest of the campus. Chaffee and Jacobson (1997) concur that frequent and open communication about change efforts can increase levels of trust across multiple campus cultures and thereby reduce resistance. Town meetings to discuss learning communities, presentations to faculty governing bodies, and a program newsletter are all methods learning communities leaders can use to keep the campus engaged and informed.

Organizational Culture

Organizational culture has been compared to a rubber band: it is flexible enough to be stretched to a new shape under force of pressure but elastic enough to spring back to its original form if the pressure is released. Looking at organizational change through a cultural lens can lead to seeing new possibilities for change. Recognizing the different values of faculty and administrative cultures raises two needs: (1) deliberative processes that reflect a faculty value of collecting and analyzing information and (2) clear decision-making processes that reflect the administrative value of setting and achieving goals. "What most institutions need to do is develop a shared culture that values and seeks change in ways that affirm fundamental commitments while letting go of their trappings" (Chaffee and Jacobson, 1997, p. 233). For some learning community programs, this may mean affirming the central value of writing to the learning process and incorporating substantial writing components into learning community courses but letting go of a course titled English Composition. For most learning communities, the cultural values that are maintained include the primacy of faculty in determining the curriculum and the importance of drawing students into deep examinations of issues from multiple perspectives.

Examining the relationships between constituent groups, breaking away from old structures and exploring new patterns, and gaining clarity on the desired purpose of the change are ways to reshape an organizational culture so that change is possible. Monitoring the progress and extent of the change and communicating openly and frequently with groups across campus help sustain innovation. If organizational change is to be compared with propelling a boat through water, then sustaining change involves the factors that keep the boat moving: fuel, steering, reducing resistance or drag, and favorable winds.

The Purposes of Learning Communities

Learning community programs can be tremendously flexible, addressing the needs of specific student populations or specific curricular issues. Too much flexibility, however, can lead to a lack of focus. Clearly defining the purpose of learning communities during implementation, and continuously revisiting the purpose(s), is essential to sustainability. Although this sounds obvious, it is often glossed over. Questions that campuses should be prepared to ask and answer, related to their motivation for implementing learning communities, include:

- Are the reasons for making this reform substantial and enduring enough to maintain its momentum throughout anticipated challenges?
- Is the purpose(s) of the learning community initiative congruent with the mission of the institution?
- Will the work required of faculty and administrators be intrinsically meaningful, at least in part?

These are difficult questions, but they are not unreasonable given the significant results that can be expected. Asking these questions acknowledges that curricular reform involves more than a new marketing angle or jumping on a trendy bandwagon, but in return, results may go beyond just improved retention rates.

Defining the purpose(s) of a learning community program begins with a series of questions as well. What are the learning goals of the program? How does the design of the program address the goals? How will achievement of the goals be measured? If the goals involve curricular change, such as increasing the use of interdisciplinary approaches in critical thinking or problem solving or increasing the level of complexity of writing assignments across the curriculum, then the design of the program needs to include how the goals will be defined within each academic course. If the learning goals involve greater student interaction with faculty (for the purposes of increased integration to the college or greater identification with a potential major, for example), then attention needs to be paid to how patterns of interaction will be influenced by the learning community program. Learning goals that relate to increased interactions among students require a learning community model that specifically structures opportunities for such interactions. Defining and clarifying goals at the outset of the program will lead to informed choices as the implementation process progresses.

Learning communities, with their intentional restructuring of the classroom and curriculum, are one model for achieving greater gains in student learning outcomes. Some learning communities, however, start with goals that are not so clearly linked to learning outcomes. These programs may need extra attention to understanding and measuring the factors that influence these goals. For example, if learning communities are started as a way to increase student retention, has the campus in question examined the reasons for lower-than-desired rates of retention? One assumption is that students leave a college because they are not engaged with the academic and social life of the campus, but what does that mean? Does it mean that students have little direct contact with faculty? Does it mean that students' curiosity is not sparked because the content of a class is similar to a like course in high school? Does it mean that students who are undeclared about their major feel less committed to the college? Are some students just plain homesick, or is the financial burden of higher education not seen as a worthwhile investment? Learning communities may be an important part of a retention plan, but if the dynamics of retention on a campus are not well understood, and if the reason for starting learning communities is to increase retention, then the "success" of the program may always be suspect or never proven.

Recall the example of Worst Case Scenario University, where concerns about poor student retention served as the impetus for creating learning communities. Without examining possible causes of poor retention at WCSU, the learning community model was likely to have been selected for another reason—the need to implement a less complex approach in a short time. Even if retention rates increased after learning communities were implemented, it would be difficult to attribute the success to the learning community program or any parts thereof, since no theoretical model had been used in choosing a learning community approach. Again, the more specific the purposes of starting a learning community program, the better the chances for implementing a program that fits well with the campus, the better the chances for assessment, and the better the chances the work can be sustained.

It should be noted that some goals may seem too ambitious to attempt, depending on the source of the change. It is unlikely that a small group of faculty could achieve a goal of reexamining the role of the liberal arts in the entire undergraduate curriculum, especially at a medium or large university. But they could meet a goal of increasing the use of experiential learning or service learning in a major field or creating a more integrated flow of courses within a particular school. The scope of some goals may actually impede the ability to clarify them and identify means of measurement. In *Experiment at Berkeley,* Joseph Tussman (1969) described the curriculum of the "first program" (which spanned the first two years of study) as "concerned with central moral, political, or social problems, . . . concerned with initiation into the great political vocation" (p. 120). He then went on to describe the difficulty in evaluating the program, knowing that in its special departure from the traditional system, the program needed even more justification for use of resources. However, he was not sure what kind of justification was needed. Learning community leadership with a broad mandate for sweeping change must be able to articulate the programs' purposes and expected outcomes in detailed, observable, and measurable ways.

Some goals may be problematic for the sustainability of an initiative. Programs developed in response to impending accreditation reviews, for example, or chiefly as a way to increase income without an understanding of the relationship between student learning and revenue cannot be expected to last. Implementing learning communities because everyone is doing it is an exercise in change for change's sake. Programs whose goals are too broad in scope can be difficult to maintain, as can programs whose goals are not far-reaching enough. The imperative of a meaningful purpose for change was summarized by a colleague who concluded that, for program implementation to be sustainable, people need to participate for reasons that are fairly permanent, not for reasons of financial exigency, accreditation, or the latest fad (D. Stearns, personal communication, December 2001).

Integration with the College or University Mission

Intertwined with the necessity of a clearly defined purpose for implementing learning communities is the importance of integrating the learning community program within the core mission of the institution. Congruence between a learning community initiative and the institution's mission is essential, since the mission relates to and influences systems such as faculty rewards, recruitment of students, and allocation of financial resources. For example, a learning community program focused on linking upper-level undergraduate students and faculty in research projects may attract and keep faculty at a research university more so than a program that tries to link first-year students with research faculty. When such a program increases the amount of research support that faculty receive, faculty can participate in learning communities without having to sacrifice work in an area that is likely to be rewarded over teaching. New faculty members at Wagner College are hired with the understanding that they will be actively involved in first-year and senior-year learning communities, and their participation is recognized in the process of promotion and tenure. This is consistent with Wagner's mission as a liberal arts college focused on the teaching of undergraduate students (R. Guarasci, personal communication, January 2002).

Achieving congruence between a learning community program and the mission of the institution may be easier than it sounds. Like the example of Worst Case Scenario University, many large universities are comprehensive in their missions. As a result, within a learning community program there may be multiple purposes for engaging in learning communities. Communities may be developed to meet the needs of smaller academic units within the institution or to support certain populations of students. At Stony Brook University, for example, learning communities take a number of shapes and designs, including living-learning communities that encompass academic minors, learning communities with transition to college seminars for first-year students, learning communities for women in science and engineering, and an Honors College (S. Sullivan and J. Stein, personal communication, October 2003).

Students are more likely to approach learning communities with a welcoming attitude if the program is consistent with their reasons for attending the college or university. If students (and parents) are told from the beginning of the recruitment process that learning communities are a part of the curriculum, and the reasons for the program are consistent with the mission of the institution, then the actual advisement and registration process is eased considerably. Advisers then are not expected to do all the work of introducing the concept of learning communities, answering questions about the particular program, convincing students and parents that it is a good thing, and finally helping the student select a learning community. In addition, the more students understand the goals of learning communities and come to expect them on their campus, the less faculty need to do as far as socializing students to the concept.

Finally, learning communities compete for financial resources with other programs on campuses. Centrality of the learning community program to the mission of the institution can have an impact on financial resource allocation in two ways. If teaching in a learning community reinforces work that faculty are expected to do, then less financial incentive will be needed to keep faculty involved. More important, if the learning community program is central to the way the mission of the college is enacted on campus, then it does not have to be repeatedly introduced and defended during annual budget deliberations. When more funding is needed to either make changes or scale up a pilot program to more students, the ability to call on the mission of the institution to justify expenses can help (Shapiro and Levine, 1999).

Stability of Campus Leadership

The leaders of any organization can be instrumental in establishing or at least shaping its culture, and institutions of higher education are no exception (Chaffee and Jacobson, 1997). Leaders who understand the importance of culture in influencing the actions of an organization's members can use their positions to send messages about the culture and to provide incentives for cultural change. In cases in which the leader has been instrumental in making change in the organization, his or her departure can jeopardize the sustainability of the change, especially if the change has not permeated the organization and has not been embraced by personnel in key positions. In a survey about creating collaborations between academic and student affairs units on campuses, it was reported that "senior administrative support was by far the most often cited variable for success, with eighty percent [of respondents] stating that it was a very successful strategy" (Kezar, Hirsch, and Burack, 2001, p. 45). Although structural and cultural strategies were cited in successful collaborations as well, influential leaders played an important role.

Learning community programs that have been in place for a fairly long time often can point to a small group of people who have been instrumental to the program's longevity. Typically, they have an administrative champion, someone who advocates for and protects program resources. This person's deep commitment to the program can provide a buffer from leadership changes higher up in the organization (D. Lebofsky, personal communication, January 2001). For example, a dean of undergraduate studies can keep a program on course in spite of frequent changes at the provost level. This type of person is important from a policy perspective as well, if they have "control" over a group of students and staff. A dean of a college, for example, can direct her advisers and faculty to participate in learning communities even if the rest of the university does not. The stability of such people in these positions influences their ability to develop and then draw upon a reservoir of goodwill when interacting with faculty and staff over the course of years (D. Stearns, personal communication, December, 2001). Relationships can be built, trust can be earned, and then energy can be spent on program development and modification rather than establishing new relationships with new leaders. Although the case of Worst Case Scenario University is fictitious, it is not uncommon for innovations to come and go with their administrative champions. The presence of a supportive leader does not guarantee the longevity of learning communities, but the absence of a supportive leader can put a significant strain on the people who are left to continue the program.

Developing a stable core of faculty is equally important for the sustainability of learning communities. Although it is important to recruit new faculty so that new ideas can be brought into a program and so that feelings of ownership are shared by larger proportions of the total faculty, a large amount of faculty turnover can be a considerable drain on the program. The time and energy spent on recruiting and training large numbers of new faculty to participate can be better spent toward program modification and fine-tuning. Faculty burnout can be an issue, but it does not always mean that faculty members need to leave the learning community program. Once a program is up and running, faculty may become invigorated by the possibilities of program evolution. Once the First-Year Program had been running for a few years at Wagner College, a group of faculty turned their attention to spreading responsibility for the improvement of students' writing in their second semester and subsequent years beyond the Languages and Literature Department.

Expansion of the Learning Community Leadership Network on Campus

Related to the need for a stable core of administrators and faculty is the need to expand the learning community leadership network on campus. Increasing the number of people committed to and responsible for a learning community program helps sustain the program even if key leaders leave or early adopters burn out.

For many years, LaGuardia Community College had a prominent champion in Roberta Matthews, who held the position of vice provost. She cultivated faculty leaders within the various program areas (for example, business, liberal arts, developmental programs). Some faculty carried reduced teaching loads in return for administrative duties such as faculty development, program development, and program assessment. They were supported in their efforts to publish and make presentations about their experiences in learning communities and subsequently have become leaders of the programs themselves. Therefore, when Roberta Matthews left LaGuardia, the stability of the programs was not jeopardized (P. VanSlyck, personal communication, October 2002).

Because the work of creating organizational change can be so labor-intensive, sharing the responsibility with others is critical to preventing burnout. Although the initial change agent may be a single individual or a small group of people, part of their job in creating change is to recruit "early adopters"–leaders among mainstream administrators and faculty who are open to new ideas and willing to try innovations (AtKisson, 1999). In the case of learning communities, the change agent may be the person(s) who brings the idea to campus, but early adopters will be the faculty who teach in the learning community program and the faculty and administrators who are involved with implementation. When Temple University's founding faculty fellow for learning communities stepped down, a new Learning Communities Associates Program was begun. Faculty members were brought in as "associates" to work on projects specific to their interests and expertise, such as assessment or faculty development. One faculty member in the Criminal Justice Department had experience with research on adolescents, and he applied research methods from his discipline to the study of students in learning communities (J. Levine Laufgraben, personal communication, April 2002).

Expansion of Buy-in Beyond Faculty

A learning community program that may start out as a faculty initiative with the goal of curricular restructuring can grow in scope to include the efforts of personnel in libraries, admissions, residence life, student activities and organizations, advising, information technology, career development, communications, and other offices or programs on campus. Each of these areas will do well to have internal advocates for learning communities–people willing to learn about new programs and new ways of thinking and to collaborate with other departments with which they may have had little previous interaction.

If program expansion continues, it could be argued that more people must be involved in the resulting challenges and that new ideas are likely to come from newer participants (Heifetz and Laurie, 1997). It is not just that more faculty will be necessary to teach more sections of courses; if the learning community program is expanded to incorporate opportunities for experiential learning or community-based learning, then more coordination will be necessary between faculty, students, and off-campus sites. For example, faculty at St. Lawrence University initiated the First-Year Program and envisioned close collaboration with the personnel responsible for residence life and academic advising. In the development of the First-Year Program, however, the need became apparent for an orientation program that was better integrated with the new curriculum. What started out as a faculty initiative expanded to include other groups on campus (S. Horwitz, personal communication, August 2002).

Successful learning community programs, by their very nature, seek to bridge the work of students and faculty, intentionally providing opportunities for integration and collaboration. It follows, then, that as programs mature and expand, opportunities for the involvement of other groups across campus not only will result but also will be necessary for the sustainability of the efforts.

Curricular Integration

The curriculum is at the center of students' and teachers' academic experiences in learning communities. Without clearly articulated curricular integration, students and faculty may be unsure of the purpose of the learning community, and therefore the work of learning community development may yield lesser outcomes. Without curricular integration, students merely are block-registered, which may allow them to get to know each other but will not foster more meaningful connections among students, teachers, and disciplines. Without faculty clearly setting curricular goals and sharing expectations with students, students may take the lead in developing the norms of the classrooms. Too often those are norms of passivity in class, resistance to meeting high expectations, and attempts to play one professor off the other ("Professor X doesn't require this in his course, why do we have to do it here?"). Curricular integration, cutting across departmental or disciplinary boundaries and looking at topics from multiple perspectives, forms the foundation of meaningful learning communities. Programs that lose sight of the central role of curriculum in "curricular" learning communities run the risk of establishing communities in name only. Curricular planning is discussed further in Chapter Three.

Sustained Faculty Development

Faculty development supports curriculum development and reinforces the active forms of pedagogy that are characteristic of learning communities. Within learning community programs, faculty development may take many forms, from the expensive and formal, such as attendance at professional conferences, to the thrifty and informal, such as pairs of faculty meeting to discuss how to integrate assignments. (Faculty development is discussed in depth in Chapter Five.) Selecting the best approach to faculty development depends on the stage of program development and the level of experience of the faculty members involved. What is most important for the sustainability of learning community programs, however, is that some form of faculty development exists and that faculty participate.

Faculty development provides exposure to new ideas and information, opportunities to work together to develop or refine an individual learning community, and chances to gain expertise in a specific aspect of program development such as assessment. It also allows emerging leaders to learn of initiatives at other institutions. Frequently, faculty refer to the opportunity to engage with their peers in discussions of teaching, rather than other aspects of the faculty role, as one of the most motivating aspects of their learning community participation (Gabelnick, MacGregor, Matthews, and Smith, 1990).

Returning to the analogy introduced in the beginning of this chapter, faculty development is the fuel needed to keep the luxury cruiser in motion—it energizes and invigorates the program. The content and process of faculty development should be planned so that it supports and guides the needs of the learning community program. In this way it becomes an essential factor in sustaining learning communities.

Availability of Resources

Faculty are key personnel resources in any learning community program. Sustained faculty development is one key ingredient of a successful learning community program. In addition to faculty, administrators play important roles in the sustenance of learning communities. As learning community programs become more complex—incorporating service learning, interdisciplinary themes, and residence life, for example—their sustainability hinges upon continued personnel and financial resources. Although learning communities involve some structures that were in place at the college or university prior to their implementation—such as courses and faculty to teach them—other components of learning communities bring new budgetary implications that should be understood as permanent. This is important especially for programs that start with grant funding. As funds from the grant are phased out, other funds from the institution are needed to replace them. Continued assessment can also help identify aspects of the program that can be modified to reduce costs without adversely affecting the outcomes.

Sustainable learning communities need funds for ongoing faculty development and funds to conduct various assessment projects. Fiscal resources, as well as staff support, may be available by partnering with existing teaching and learning centers or an office of institutional research. In addition, depending on the features of the program, funds may be required for out-of-class activities, field trips, research projects, events or fairs highlighting and celebrating the work of students and faculty, or for external speakers or performers.

Indeed, the notion of sustainability does not imply that a system can be started and then left to run forever without infusions of resources. Rather, sustainability involves maintenance. This may mean the need for reallocation of resources instead of adding more resources. For example, with the advent of the Wagner Plan, Wagner College no longer hired adjunct professors to teach freshman composition courses. Although some of that money went to hire adjuncts to supplement other academic departments, some went to support the Writing Center and peer writing intensive tutors, who in turn could support first-year students in their writing development.

Partnering with other departments on campus may enable conservation of fiscal resources as well. If faculty want to invite guest speakers, they may be able to go to an office of co-curricular programs or a student activities office for funding as well as logistical help, especially if all students can be invited to attend. Other offices or departments to consider when seeking cosponsors for campus events are residence life, health services, athletics, career development, and alumni relations.

What is most salient in a discussion of personnel and financial resources is the extent to which those resources are used effectively in the achievement of the program goals. Judgments of effectiveness involve measures of resource expenditure and goal achievement and as such necessitate comprehensive assessment efforts.

Assessment

Implementation of learning communities can only progress so far before people on campus, both within and out of the program, ask, "How's it going?" Program assessment can take many forms, from a head count of students to an examination of the development of writing skills. In the beginning stages of program development, the assessment may focus on nuts and bolts of implementation such as the effectiveness of recruitment of students and faculty to the program, student and faculty perceptions of the interactions in the communities, or student and faculty understanding of the purpose of the innovation. As programs evolve, assessment turns to questions of student learning outcomes, faculty development outcomes, and other indicators that the programs are achieving their goals. One impediment to sustaining reform on campus is that assessment gets overlooked in the planning and early implementation phases (Tierney, 2001).

An active assessment program must be understood as one that completes a feedback loop to a variety of stakeholder audiences. Information that can be used toward improving the program can be important to internal audiences such as faculty and various administrators. External audiences such as parents, other administrators, trustees, public officials, and accreditors may require information that can demonstrate proof of achievement of program goals. Lack of assessment results, or the lack of communication about assessment results, will jeopardize change efforts. Critics may point to the lack of information as proof that learning communities do not work. People open to learning about the innovation will want some demonstration of its effectiveness in order to be persuaded to support it.

A final point about assessment and ongoing program development is that often the new programs on campus are the only programs being assessed. If new programs have come about with the help of a grant, reports are required to complete the funding process. Programs that have been in existence for a long time, however, may not receive the same level of scrutiny or may cease to conduct regular assessment when resources are no longer available. Ongoing assessment is central to sustaining learning communities, and assessment should be planned alongside routine program decisions such as scheduling and recruiting students. Assessment is examined in depth in Chapter Six.

Conclusion

This chapter has introduced a number of topics and issues that are critical for program implementation *and* sustainability. Key to sustainability, however, are the factors that keep learning communities central to the mission of the institution, that cultivate leadership and ownership by many people in different areas, and that identify, recognize, and reward behaviors congruent with the continued development of the program(s). The size of the program is not as important as its purpose(s) and the clarity with which those purposes are articulated. In addition, it is important to operationalize the program goals, identify indicators of progress, measure the indicators (collect data), and communicate the data back to key audiences. This may mean different things at different points in the life of the program: early in the development of learning communities on a campus it may be important to gather feedback for purposes of program improvement, whereas later, data may be necessary for proving the results and justifying continued use of resources.

Program sustainability need not mean that the same or original model of learning community is always in place on a campus. Being flexible with learning community models and adapting them to meet the needs of a campus, while at the same time maintaining overall program quality, may ultimately result in learning communities that are embedded in the culture of the institution. Variations in the targeted audience, the type of model, and the types of pedagogy practiced in the learning communities allow for learning communities to be shaped to fit the gamut of institutional types.

Integrating the purposes of the learning community program with the mission of the institution is like choosing the right kind of boat for your voyage—not starting out on an ocean voyage in a rowboat, for instance. In addition, it is important to have a captain to steer the course (stability of leadership), recruit and train an able crew and officers (expanding the leadership network on campus), and use navigational aides such as radar and wind speed and direction indicators to keep the ship on course (program assessment).

CHAPTER THREE

PLANNING AND ASSESSING THE CURRICULUM

Curriculum development is the primary responsibility of faculty, so it follows that faculty teaching in learning communities will design and develop the curriculum for their communities. The extent to which students will experience an integrated or interdisciplinary learning environment depends on a sustained curricular planning process. It begins with setting shared goals for curricular outcomes and common expectations for student learning. Designing a curricular plan involves decisions about content, process, outcomes, and alignment. The effectiveness of this plan is determined through assessing student learning and redesigning the curriculum to ensure student learning goals are met. The role of program leadership is to provide faculty development opportunities and provide teachers with adequate time and resources for presemester and academic-year curriculum planning and ongoing assessment and revision.

A quality undergraduate curriculum is characterized by coherence, synthesizing experiences, ongoing practice of learned skills, and integration of education and experience. Research on curriculum shows that the following conditions foster the development of college-level competencies:

- Challenging courses
- Supportive environments
- Active involvement in learning

- High expectations
- Clearly defined and attainable goals
- Frequent assessment and prompt feedback (Diamond, 1998)

From learning community models that link two courses to the more interdisciplinary, team-taught approaches, students and teachers embrace commonalities and differences and engage in much more active learning than typically found in discretely taught general education courses. Creating the kinds of active, collaborative classrooms exemplified by learning communities requires an investment in curricular planning prior to the semester or quarter, as well as ongoing dialogue between the teachers and students in the community.

Curriculum Planning in Learning Communities

On many campuses, curriculum planning begins in the proposal stage of learning communities. If the program is set up so that faculty teaching teams independently propose a learning community, the proposal form or process should include questions on curricular design. For example, the Cluster Proposal Form used by LaGuardia Community College asks several questions about course organization:

1. What central question or theme will the cluster explore?
2. How will each course differ from its "stand-alone" version?
3. How will specific classroom activities in each discipline contribute to the exploration of the cluster's central themes?

If the learning communities offered are scheduled with minimal faculty input and faculty are then recruited to teach in the program, curricular planning can be more challenging. Faculty development should provide sufficient resources and time for presemester planning. Consider developing a curriculum planning document that faculty teaching teams can complete prior to the start of the semester. (Faculty development is discussed in Chapter Five.)

The Community Plan Worksheet used by Temple University Learning Communities teachers is one such tool. The plan is part of the faculty handbook distributed to faculty when they are assigned to teach a course in a learning community. Faculty meet as a team to discuss the plan, and each person receives a stipend when the plan is submitted. Exhibit 3.1 is the community plan for a learning community linking an introductory women's studies course with college composition.

Regardless of the model(s) of learning communities on your campus, some general curricula planning principles apply:

1. Set goals for student learning.
2. Determine content.
3. Consider instructional approaches.
4. Consider students' entire learning experiences.
5. Develop structures for assessing curricula effectiveness.
6. Plan opportunities to review and redesign the "community curriculum."

Set Goals for Student Learning

Discussing and agreeing upon learning goals and objectives is an important first step in the process of developing the curriculum for learning communities. The conversation begins with learning about each other's courses and disciplines and progresses to clarifying the goals and objectives for the community. Develop meaningful, clear, and realistic goals for student learning at the course or program (community) level. In its publication, *Student Learning Assessment: Options and Resources,* the Middle States Commission on Higher Education (2003) suggests the following when selecting learning goals:

- Start with success (determine what learning goals are already being assessed and what data might be available).
- Ensure relevance of goals.
- Choose goals that can lead to improvement.
- Emphasize higher-order thinking skills.
- Define learning goals before choosing assessment methods (operationally define each goal and tailor data collection to defined goals) [p. 20].

When considering the goals and objectives for the community, take into account the goals and objectives of the individual courses and disciplines and their alignment. Consider the following questions as you move from a discussion of courses to community: (1) What is the role of each course in the curriculum? (2) Are other instructors relying on this course to provide specific background knowledge of skills? (3) How are your students different or alike? (McKeachie, 2002).

EXHIBIT 3.1. TEMPLE UNIVERSITY COMMUNITY PLAN

Community Plan Worksheet
CO76: American Women's Lives, Section 601, 025059
CO50: College Composition, Section 626, 061002

LC Title: "Writing Projects: Public Writing, Private Agency"

1. What central questions or themes will your learning community explore?
Themes include: feminism, gender, sexuality, self-expression, agency, and activism. Questions include: What are the assumptions that an author makes about her audience? How do we make meaning out of our lives through the discourses available to us? What do women writers believe about self-expression, identity, and public responsibility? What are the ways in which, and to what extent, student writing and action can be responsible to both private and public concerns?

2. How will the individual courses integrate the theme for this learning community?
In the women's studies course, students will read about women from a range of ethnicities, races, classes, sexualities, and regions of the country. Texts will include autobiography, short-story, novel, drawings, narrative film, documentary film, letters, essays, diaries, and photos. In the composition class, students will be challenged to identify and develop both a central problem/concern as it pertains to their own lives/experience and an understanding of public needs surrounding gender, women, and sexuality. The two classes will share a focus on issues concerning gender, issues of femininity, masculinity, the personal and public, sexuality, and local activism.

3. What pedagogical strategies will be implemented to promote the integration of knowledge?
Both classes will incorporate small-group work, class discussion, guest speakers, partnered presentations, peer review, student-teacher conferences, (overlapping) challenging readings, and out-of-classroom activities.

4. In what ways will the LC support students' transition to college-level learning?
Above all, the instructors will confer once a week to discuss our students' progress, taking action immediately to support students who may need various types of support. Students will be supported in their transition to college-level learning by a variety of means, such as thorough handouts regarding the coursework/assignments, a variety of types of assignments (to allow for different learning styles), our help with their internet research, an interactive classroom with small-group work, class discussions, guest speakers, partnered oral presentations, peer review/student feedback on student writing, topics that overlap in both courses, and out-of-classroom activities. We will, as instructors, also have extra availability outside of the classroom: regular student/teacher conferences, extra office hours for consultation on projects, and contact by e-mail. In both classes, students will work together in group projects; students and teachers will go to events out of class; there will be group e-mails to the students, keeping them informed of future work and important reminders; and students are encouraged to contact the instructors out of class by e-mail.

5. In what ways will this LC experience enhance connections between and among students and teachers?

We hope that the comfortable, supportive environment we create in the classroom (see answers to above question) forms a unique community of students and teachers committed to self-expression and public responsibility. We encourage our students to make friends in class and to think of this community experience as an opportunity to create relationships that they will continue to call on throughout their college careers, including calling on their teachers for advice and letters of recommendation, etc.

6. If your learning community includes a section of the first-year seminar, how do you plan to incorporate the seminar in terms of advancing the curricular theme?

Not applicable.

7. What skills or knowledge should students acquire as a result of their participation in this learning community?

The goals of our learning community are for our students to become fluent and powerful critical thinkers, readers, speakers, researchers, and writers. They will also gain a significant knowledge of women's lives, historical contexts, and women writers. Students in the Women's Studies class will work on writing their own autobiographies and writing the biography of another, older woman's life. In the composition class, students will learn about local activism, how to develop a project for change, and how to investigate their own concerns.

8. How will you assess student progress in terms of the outcomes described above?

Students will be required to make presentations, participate in class, and submit papers (including autobiography, responses, reflection, and academic writing). Instructors will provide critical feedback and letter grades (on certain work), hold one-on-one conferences with students, and ask students to assess their own experiences at various points throughout the semester.

According to Mager (1975, p. 21), instructional objectives should have three characteristics. The first is performance: what the learner is expected to be able to do. The second characteristic is conditions: the conditions under which the performance is to take place. The third characteristic is the criterion on which performance will be evaluated: how well must the learner perform? Objectives should be written in clear, specific language that communicates the educational intent of the learning community.

A learning community at the University of Texas at San Antonio (UTSA) entitled "Revolutions and Revelations: Buried Treasures in Your Own Backyard" links Texas history, freshman composition, and a freshman seminar. The teachers describe their community as a journey: "This course's journey will be as much fun as its destination. To unearth the 'buried treasures' of their new word power, students will take several real-life trips into Texas' past via videos, visits to restaurants, museums, cemeteries, even archival 'excavations.' Along the way, incidental rewards will include exciting new international friends, both past and present" (http://www.utsa.edu/lc/schedule/schedule.cfm?s=Fall&y =2002).

The Texas history syllabus outlines the curricular objectives in terms of both knowledge acquisition and skill development:

> This course provides students the opportunity to learn about topics and trends in Texas history from the earliest appearance of Indian communities in the region to the November 2002 statewide elections. Important themes in-clude the affect of environment on life in Texas, community development, the contest of empires, race and gender as sources of cooperation and conflict, economic transformations, and the nature of Texas politics. As we explore these themes we will study the Alamo, cowboys, oil wells, Willie Nelson, and the other aspects of Texas life that have contributed to the state's mystique.
>
>   In addition to learning about Texas history, students will have the oppor-tunity to improve learning skills. We will work on analyzing and critically evaluating ideas, arguments, and points of view. We will discuss the best ways to learn from monographs (books written on a particular subject). Finally, several assignments will give you the opportunity to improve your writing [http://www.utsa.edu/lc/syllabi/fall2002/his2053701.cfm].

A learning community at Temple University entitled "African-American Experience in Philadelphia" linked an African American history course, college composition, and a freshman seminar. As a community, students and teachers explored the following questions: What role have African Americans played in Philadelphia's history? From a sociopolitical perspective, how has Philadelphia accepted or dealt with the African American community? What role has culture played in shaping the history of Philadelphia? Does culture affect how society interprets history and texts? What is the current state of affairs for African Americans in Philadelphia? On their community plan, the teachers for this community outlined the learning tasks and objectives for students: "The central themes of the courses will be the nature of Philadelphia's rich African American history. Students will be asked to investigate and reevaluate their views regarding Philadelphia's history through essays, group presentations, handouts, current events, class discussion and textbooks. Students will analyze Philadelphia's diverse history through an African-centered perspective and be asked to think critically about this theoretical framework. Students should become more comfortable with expressing their ideas and opinions through writing and speaking. They will also obtain a greater knowledge of African

American history through critical, in-depth analysis" (A. McKinnon, personal communication, July 2003).

Determine Content

According to Wiggins and McTigh (1998), an important step in curricular planning is considering "the curricular activities and teachings—the design work at the heart of everyday teaching" (p. 98). They advocate for "uncoverage," going beyond simply covering content and "inquiring into, around and underneath content" (p. 98). In learning communities students need to not only learn about various subjects but also about the relationships between these disciplines and how this content transfers to other learning and life experiences. In determining content it is important to ask: "What is worthy and requiring of understanding?" (p. 99).

The nature and extent of content decisions depends on the learning community models. In student cohorts in large classes (freshman interest groups, FIGs), content is not intentionally integrated. Students enroll in discretely taught courses for which there is no expectation of team planning. Students discuss content in weekly seminars. In linked-course learning communities, content is related or, more optimally, integrated. Teachers develop a "community curriculum" by discussing ways to connect content across the discretely taught courses. It is in team-taught learning communities that discussions about content are the most involved, since it is the responsibility of the multidisciplinary teaching teams to create the curriculum for the community.

Regardless of the model, discussions of content can be one of the most difficult tasks in the curricular planning process. The issue of depth versus breadth is likely to arise when teachers come together to discuss the content requirements of their courses or disciplines. This can be particularly problematic in communities that include introductory courses to majors, courses in which the faculty member is expected to lay the curricular foundation for more advanced learning in the discipline. Wiggins and McTigh (1998) offer the following advice: "The challenge in blending depth and breadth in design of curriculum and instruction is to ensure that the ratio is properly balanced for the topic and time allotted. This effort naturally involves choices, compromises and sacrifices that play off the overarching priorities, standards and student abilities and interests" (p. 101). If the faculty teaching in learning communities do not have a clear and common understanding for the expectations for curricular integration, and there are not the opportunities and structures to support them in this planning process, the result is likely to be either inconsistencies across communities in terms of the quality of the curriculum or experiences for students that are more social than academic.

Consider Instructional Approaches

In early curriculum planning discussions, teaching teams need to discuss not only what will be taught but how it will be taught. Diamond (1998) suggests considering the following factors when discussing instructional approaches: (1) the specific learning outcomes you want to reach, (2) the research on learning, and (3) available instructional options, including the structure of the course (lecture, small group activities, and so on) (p. 153). In *Designing and Assessing Courses and Curricula,* Diamond (1998) summarizes the research on instructional approaches and learning. Findings include

- Active learning is more effective than passive learning.
- Teaching is more effective when the instructional methods used take into account the diverse ways students learn.
- Changes in students' ability to think critically are significantly and positively correlated with levels of praise from faculty, interaction among students and faculty, and high-level cognitive responses from students in class.
- To be remembered, new information must be meaningfully connected to prior knowledge, and it must be remembered in order to be learned.
- High expectations encourage high achievement.
- Students tend to routinely use study methods that are known not to work (such as reading textbooks) and must be taught how to learn effectively [pp. 156–157].

Many students enter the learning community classroom(s) with high expectations. They expect livelier, interactive classrooms where they will get to know and work collaboratively with their peers. In developing their curricular plan, teachers should consider the pedagogical approaches characteristic of a learning community classroom, including discussion, labs, experiential learning, collaborative learning, writing across the curriculum, group activities and assignments, case study methods, even lectures. (Pedagogy is discussed further in the next chapter.) Discuss with students, early in the semester, the instructional approaches that will be incorporated into the community and expectations for what it means to learn in community. Specifically, what are the roles and responsibilities of the students as learners?

Consider Students' Entire Learning Experiences

Not all learning occurs in the classroom. When developing the curriculum for a learning community, consider students' entire learning experiences and not only opportunities for learning within the classroom. Consider experiential learning activities, service projects, internships, field trips, or campus activities that might deepen students' understanding of course and community concepts.

In the General Education Clusters at UCLA, teaching teams incorporate out-of-class learning experiences to support curricular objectives. In the "Global Environment Cluster," students are required to participate in one field trip in the fall and winter quarters. Students can choose from a variety of sites: the Los Angeles River, the Bellona wetlands, UCLA Stunt Ranch, the Tillman Water Reclamation Plant, Santa Monica Bay, the UCLA energy facility, a toxic tour of Los Angeles, an urban sprawl tour of Ventura County, or the Palm Springs windmills. Social activities that help students get to know their peers and teachers include barbecues and gatherings in the residential life area (G. Kendrick, personal communication, April 2003).

In the UCLA "Frontiers in Human Aging Cluster," all 120 students engage in service learning during the winter quarter. Students are placed for five weeks at age-oriented organizations or programs in the Los Angeles area, such as retirement homes, the Geriatric Center at the UCLA Medical Center, and social welfare agencies. Students conduct in-depth studies of the agencies while interacting with their clientele.

Many learning community programs redesign traditional classrooms or create classroom spaces in residence halls so the learning space reflects the goals and intended outcomes of learning communities. Learning communities classes can also meet in outdoor field sites or at off-campus locations with resources and facilities to advance the community or program theme. For example, students in UCLA's 2003–2004 "Performing Arts Cluster" will spend about half the winter quarter at the Getty Institute "studying various objects in the five major collections of the museum with an eye aimed at learning how the political, social and aesthetic philosophy of five different historical periods is embodied in that period's musical and dramatic performance" (G. Kendrick, personal communication, April 2003).

Assess Curricula Effectiveness

The expectation of student engagement in learning takes on a new dimension in today's climate of institutional accountability, which requires campuses to demonstrate evidence of student learning. Again, learning communities are front and center in producing evidence of student engagement. Good curriculum planning is guided by questions routinely asked by those in assessment: "What should our students know?" and "What skills should they command?" (Wright, 2000, pp. 299–300). A third question that needs to be asked in order to assess curriculum effectiveness is, "How do we measure the extent to which students are meeting or have met these content and skill objectives?"

At the community level, assessment of student learning outcomes can contribute to the discussion of overall curricula effectiveness. Chapter Six discusses assessing the success of learning communities in more detail, but since assessment and evaluation of student learning is such an integral part of the curriculum planning process, it is also discussed here. "Equally important, if we are to be successful as teachers we must be sure that the goals we have developed are being reached by our students and that assumptions we are making about them are accurate" (Diamond, 1998, pp. 139–140). Along with decisions about goals and instructional strategies, learning community teaching teams should also consider ways to assess student performance and instructional effectiveness.

Evaluating student learning can include indirect or direct measures that provide either quantitative or qualitative data. Both types of data provide useful information on learning outcomes. "Direct and indirect methods of evaluating learning relate to whether or not the method provides evidence in form of student products or performances. Such evidence demonstrates that actual learning has occurred relating to a specific content or skill. Indirect methods reveal characteristics associated with learning, but they only imply that learning has occurred. These characteristics may relate to the student, such as perceptions of student learning, or they may relate to the institution, such as graduation rates" (Middle States Commission on Higher Education, 2003, p. 28).

At the course level, direct measures of student learning include exams and quizzes, term papers, research projects, class discussion participation, artistic products and performance, and grades based on clear criteria related to defined learning goals. Indirect measures could include course evaluations, amount of time students spend on homework, and time spent on service projects. Across the community, direct measures might include capstone projects and student presentations. Focus groups and student surveys are two indirect measures of student learning (Middle States Commission on Higher Education, 2003).

According to Diamond (1998), course-related assessments can serve four purposes:

- Identifying students for remediation or exemption
- Determining whether objectives are being met by measuring student performance
- Determining whether and how students' attitudes toward the courses and the discipline(s) or field(s) have changed
- Determining whether the overall course design and the materials and procedures are efficient and effective [pp. 141–142].

Not all course-related assessment needs to be faculty driven. Consider ways to involve students as partners in both the learning and assessment processes.

Weimer (2002) summarizes the purposes of evaluation in the classroom as (1) enhancing the potentials to promote learning and (2) giving students opportunities to develop self- and peer-assessment skills (p. 125). The type of learner-centered evaluation that Weimer describes can focus students on learning as a process, reduce student anxiety about evaluations (tests, grades, amount of work), and allow for more useful and appropriate feedback. "In learner-centered teaching, faculty still evaluate and grade student work, but evaluation activities that involve students are included in the process; students learn how to assess their own work and participate in the evaluation of work done by their peers" (p. 119).

In the "Business Learning Communities" at Syracuse University, students complete a team project. The goals for the project are for students to learn to work in teams while enhancing their interpersonal and communication skills. In addition, the team project provides students a sense of responsibility and accountability for their own learning (S. Hurd, personal communication, April 2003). Student learning is assessed in several ways. The overall effectiveness of the team is evaluated based on the various products the team produces–written assignments, oral presentations, and the team meeting reports that each group submits after each meeting. Group performance is also evaluated through classroom observation of team exercises.

Students are active participants in the assessment process. As stated in the course handbook:

> An important tool for team learning is assessment. Two types of assessment should be used–self-assessment and team assessment. Each team member assesses her or his own behavior during team meetings by filling out, before each meeting is adjourned, a team meeting self-analysis form. This form is for the team member's own use in monitoring her or his team skills. Team assessment happens in several ways. One way is through the peer facilitator, who will share her or his observations about the team at the weekly team meeting. After the peer facilitator has shared these observations with the team, the team discusses how they worked together and establishes objectives for improving their effectiveness. Another way in which the team assesses its performance is through the team member evaluation, which will be completed online periodically throughout the semester. Your professor will provide you with a summary of the evaluations to use as a basis for improving your team process [S. Hurd, personal communication, April 2003].

Peer facilitators are upper-class, former learning communities students who apply to be peer facilitators. The Human Resources Department trains the peers in observation and feedback techniques. The peers use a checklist and an "observing task and maintenance roles" chart (see Exhibit 3.2) to observe the teams (Hurd and Richardson, 2002). In addition to feedback from the peer facilitators, teams also receive feedback from their teachers on the written and oral components of the project.

EXHIBIT 3.2. QUICK REFERENCE OBSERVATION CHECKLIST, SYRACUSE UNIVERSITY

Organization

> All working on common, explicit agenda?
> Who sits where?

Participation

> Who talks to whom?
> Who looks to whom?
> Who most frequently participates?
> What is the effect of his or her participation?
> Who participates least frequently?
> What is the effect of his or her lack of participation?
> Are there shifts in participation? What causes these?
> How are "silent" and "noisy" members handled?

Conflict

> What do members do when they disagree?
> Do people appear to take arguments in the team personally?
> Are conflicts addressed, ignored, or escalated? To what effect?

Processing

> Does the group do a self-diagnosis of its process?
> Do the members teach each other or just get the task done?
> • Who takes on the role of the teacher?
> Who fills which role?
> • Facilitator?
> • Leader?
> • Concern over process?
> • Concern over content?
> • Does it change throughout the meeting?
> • Over several meetings?
> Under what unspoken norms is the team apparently operating?
> Who takes care of task and maintenance activities?
> • Do team members make suggestions as to the best way to proceed?
> • Do members give or ask for information, opinions, feelings, and feedback or indicate that they are searching for alternatives?
> • How is the team kept on task?
> • Are all ideas presented and discussed before evaluation begins?
> • Does the team summarize what has been covered?
> • Does the team review who is responsible for doing what, when team members inputs are due, or when the team will meet again? How?

- Are all team members encouraged to enter into the discussion?
- Are there attempts by any team members to help others clarify their ideas?
- Are team members careful to reject ideas, not people?
- Are conflicts among members ignored or addressed in some way?

Decision making

How does the group go about making a decision?
Who has the most impact on the team's actions and decisions?
Whose ideas are ignored? What is the result?
What tactics do members use to influence one another?

Internal team processes
Communication
Influence
Task
Maintenance functions
Decision making
Conflict
Atmosphere
Emotional issues

Source: Hurd and Richardson, 2002, p. 27. Used by permission.

The team assessment tools provide faculty with important information on student learning and team effectiveness. According to Sandy Hurd, Faculty Coordinator for Learning Communities and Faculty in the Management Learning Community, the assessment tools provide information on

- What students don't understand about teams in a theoretical sense
- What students don't understand about teams in a behavioral sense
- What individual students are struggling with in their team experience
- When we need to provide additional support and guidance to a team or individual team member
- To what extent an individual student is realistic about the contribution he or she is making to the team
- The extent to which students understand our academic expectations [S. Hurd, personal communication, April 2003]

Many teachers are not comfortable or trained to assess student learning beyond the traditional tool box of papers, quizzes, and tests. Implementing course-related assessment, however, does not necessarily require starting from scratch. Sources of support for developing course-related assessments include

- Campus-based teaching and learning centers
- Faculty development workshops
- Colleagues in the department
- Conferences and meetings on teaching, learning, and assessment
- Guidelines disseminated by professional associations, disciplinary organizations, or accrediting bodies
- Literature on classroom assessment and research
- Opportunities to review and redesign the curriculum

Presemester curriculum planning happens in the context of ideal or "best-case" scenarios. Implementing the curriculum happens in the context of faculty and student realities. Consider the curricular plan flexible. The semester schedule or curriculum might need to be altered because students do not enter the community with the anticipated levels of knowledge or preparation, certain lessons or activities may require more time than allotted, or the schedule might be disrupted because of unforeseen current or campus events. Or perhaps the syllabus cannot be followed down to the minute because students regularly engage in rich, intellectually stimulating conversations about connections between the disciplines.

If the learning community weekly schedule does not include time for faculty planning or meetings, teachers should establish a plan for regularly communicating in person or via e-mail to discuss student learning. Meet to discuss student work, student attitudes and behavior, and perceptions of how students are experiencing the curriculum and learning community environment. In linked or clustered courses, discuss opportunities to visit each other's classes.

Program leadership should clearly articulate expectations for ongoing planning and discussion for teaching teams. At Temple, teaching teams are encouraged to complete a learning community midsemester report (Exhibit 3.3). Modeled after the community plan that teams submit prior to the start of the semester, the midsemester report is an opportunity for teams to reflect on how they and their students are experiencing the community. The questions require teaching teams to assess their progress toward meeting the curricular goals they set for their community and the stated goals for Temple's learning communities program: integration of knowledge, transition to college-level learning, and creation of connections between and among students and teachers.

Effective Learning Communities Curriculum

Curriculum planning is a process, one that can be difficult for both new and established programs. This chapter concludes with examples of learning communities that approach curriculum and instruction in different and innovative ways. Across these examples is advice for any learning communities program looking to improve curricular effectiveness. First, commit to planning as an ongoing process that involves human and fiscal resources (for example, release time, stipends, faculty development). Second, align learning community curricular objectives with degree requirements and institutional expectations for student learning. Third, be intentional in the design and delivery of the curriculum. Disciplinary connections should be explicit and clear to students in different ways–instruction, readings, and assignments–and across the courses or disciplines in the community. Fourth, make planning inclusive. Involve advisers, librarians, residence life staff, and others to partner in the curricular design process. Finally, incorporate opportunities to regularly gather faculty and student feedback on the learning experience and use this information to revisit curricular goals and design.

Intentional curricular planning and assessment can result in a learning communities curriculum that is centered upon a common set of goals and objectives that in turn form the blueprint for the types of active and deeper learning described earlier in this chapter. Broader curricular goals of learning communities might include enhancing general education, integrating study in the major or professional preparation with other disciplines, or promoting information literacy.

Enhancing General Education

The General Education Clusters in UCLA's College of Letters and Science consist of yearlong, collaboratively taught courses focusing on a timely and relevant topic. Recent themes include "The History of Modern Thought," "Evolution of the Cosmos and Life, Work, Labor and Social Justice in the U.S.," and "The Global Environment: A Multidisciplinary Perspective." Clusters are "designed to strengthen the intellectual skills of entering freshmen, introduce them to faculty research work, and expose them to such 'best practices' in teaching as seminars and interdisciplinary study" (GE Cluster Program website, http://www.college.ucla.edu/ge/clusters/). In the first two quarters, students enroll in clusters composed of lecture courses and smaller discussion or lab sections. In the spring quarter, students select from seminar offerings related to the cluster themes. Each cluster consists of 120 to 160 freshmen and a teaching cohort of three to four faculty members and three to six graduate student instructors. Clusters also feature an instructional support network of academic administrators, librarians, writing consultants, and residential life staff (G. Kendrick, personal communication, April 2003).

EXHIBIT 3.3. THE LEARNING COMMUNITIES AT TEMPLE UNIVERSITY MIDSEMESTER COMMUNITY REPORT

Semester:

Teacher	Department	Course	Campus Phone	E-mail

Learning Community Title (Theme)_____

Please look back at your community plan worksheet developed at the beginning of the semester and discuss the following questions in light of the progress made up to this point in the semester. The intention of this midsemester meeting is to give everyone a chance to get together and talk about how things are going in your learning community.

1. Given the original goals of your learning community, what do you think has worked well? What has not worked so well ? What is still left to be done?

2. In what ways have your classes been integrated thus far? How successful do you feel these integrations have been? What are you planning for the future (examples: visiting classes, team teaching, assigning the same reading, same writing assignment)?

3. If there is a freshman seminar attached to your community, in what way has the seminar been incorporated into the learning community? How has this incorporation worked in terms of advancing the goals and curricular theme of your community?

4. In what ways, if any, have your students demonstrated knowledge that they are part of a learning community (examples: direct reference to the learning community, use of materials from other classes, references to other professors)?

5. Are there students that need additional help or support in doing well in your classes? In what ways can the learning community help these students (examples: discussion of student behavior by instructors, keeping track of absences, e-mail or other contact)?

6. What have the instructors in the community done to facilitate cross-disciplinary learning in the classes? What other things could the instructors do?

UCLA's General Education Clusters evolve over a nine- to twelve-month planning period involving two phases. During phase I, five or more faculty from different disciplines form a cluster "affinity group" to organize a cluster around a particular group. The affinity group selects a cluster coordinator, who in phase II of the planning process will work with the affinity group and program administrators to formally develop a cluster proposal. Once a cluster is approved, the teaching team is selected and the more detailed curriculum planning process begins: familiarizing team members with disciplinary backgrounds, research interests, and teaching goals; developing the syllabus and assignments; and planning co-curricular learning experiences (field trips, coordinating with residential life) (G. Kendrick, personal communication, April 2003).

Students in the "Interracial Dynamics in American Culture, Society, and Literature" cluster explore the question of race in America from the disciplinary perspectives of history, law, literature, and African and Asian American studies. This cluster has been offered several times. Each time it is collaboratively taught by a teaching team of faculty drawn from the School of Law, the History and English departments, and the college's interdepartmental programs in African and Asian American studies. Participants in the 2002–2003 "Interracial Dynamics" cluster "will examine a series of cultural texts (novels, essays, films, memoirs, and scholarly works) and explore the social, political, and economical influences represented and scrutinized by them. These texts will include works by a wide array of intellectuals and artists who have addressed the question of race in American society, for example, Toni Morrison, Luis Rodriguez, bell hooks, Claudia Butler, Edward Bunker, Ruben Marinez, Chandra Mohanty and Mike Davis" (http://www.college.ucla.edu/ge/clusters/2002–2003/20abc.htm).

College Park Scholars (CPS) at the University of Maryland at College Park is a program of twelve living-learning programs for academically talented first-year and second-year students. Each faculty-designed program focuses on a particular interdisciplinary theme with a two-year curricula that fulfill general education core requirements. The College Park Scholars curriculum was designed with general education learning outcomes in mind: effective communication skills (both written and oral), quantitative literacy and analytical reasoning, appreciation of diversity, and the ability to approach unstructured problems. The twelve programs include

- Advocates for Children
- American Cultures
- Arts
- Business, Society, and the Economy
- Earth, Life, and Time

- Environmental Studies
- International Studies
- Life Sciences
- Media, Self, and Society
- Public Leadership
- Science Discovery and the Universe
- Science, Technology, and Society (Shapiro, 2003)

CPS faculty directors design curriculum around two key principles: interdisciplinarity and coherence. A critical part of the curricular planning process is helping students make academic choices. The university offers approximately five thousand courses. CPS faculty in each program carefully sift through the possible distribution requirements, match them with courses offered during a given semester, and then make strategic recommendations to students about core courses. For example, students in the Advocates for Children program are guided to choose among the foundational courses that will help them understand some of the interdisciplinary themes that arise when dealing with children's issues: psychology, sociology, children's literature, American history, economics, and so forth. The program director narrows the list of choices and then designs a colloquium (freshman seminar) to provide coherence for the intentional array of courses.

The one-credit colloquium course, which is required each semester for four semesters, serves as the synthesis point for examining cross-disciplinary texts, lectures, and research. The colloquium and the theme-specific English composition course in the first year are intentionally designed to emphasize the coherence of an interdisciplinary approach to complex topics. For example, in the colloquium for the Science, Technology, and Society program, the following topics might be discussed: transportation in the twenty-first century; new digital technologies; science, religion, and belief; biotechnology; and "Is Space a Safe Place?" (www.scholars.umd.edu).

Integrating Study in the Major or Professional Preparation with Other Disciplines

The College of Engineering at Drexel installed learning communities into its freshman and sophomore curricula to dramatically change its approach to the content and delivery of engineering education. The three-course humanities sequence taken in the first year integrates humanities with engineering subjects. Humanities and Engineering Design and Lab (ED&L) faculty collaboratively plan assignments.

In the first quarter, students complete an engineering artifacts assignment. Students select an artifact (examples: telephones, hybrid cars, global positioning systems) and then imagine what it would be like five to twenty years in the future. They are then asked to apply engineering principles to explore changes they envision for their artifacts. In the humanities course, students write poems about their artifacts and conduct research on how the objects might change. The assignment is intended to foster creativity and enhance students' abilities to understand engineering artifacts. The teaching team for the community combines lecture time for the poetry readings. Projects are graded for both engineering and humanities skills (V. Arms, personal communication, April 2003).

Additional engineering and humanities concepts are explored across the community. In the humanities course, students are required to attend and write about a play in production at an area theater. The goal is for them to see and understand roles for engineers in the arts: architectural design, lighting and sound production, or transportation. Students read literature throughout the year, including some novels with a science-fiction theme. There is a required custom-published textbook, *Humanities for the Engineering Curriculum,* that includes: (1) a course overview and schedule along with information about the campus Writing Center, (2) information on assignments, (3) the Design Project Handbook, (4) guidelines for peer review of writing, and (5) readings on technical writing, professional communication, and museum-going. In the second and third quarters, students complete a design project that is also a collaborative humanities and ED&L assignment. This project is discussed later in this chapter as an example of learning communities curricula that promote information literacy.

Students are valued members of this engineering community and are provided regular opportunities to share their concerns with the faculty team leaders through "quality circles." Quality circles, held weekly, are open forums for students to meet with team leaders to discuss how their classes and projects are progressing. At the beginning of the year, in the humanities course, students volunteer to serve as student representatives. Student representatives regularly attend the quality circles, but the forums are open to any student in the program. Sessions are not always well-attended, but they are still an opportunity for the teachers to discuss content, process, and student progress and to remind all involved in the community that quality matters.

At Portland State University, learning in the major is enhanced through student participation in interdisciplinary Senior Inquiry courses. Senior Inquiry, or SINQ, is a complementary, capstone experience to the freshman inquiry learning communities that entering students take in the first year. Senior Inquiry courses consist of students from different majors coming together with a faculty facilitator and community partners to work on substantial community projects.

Students apply the learning from their majors and from the University Studies general education curriculum to their projects. Engineering students take a particular capstone, but other seniors can select from any capstone that meets their intellectual and career interests. For example, a science major might select a capstone that is science-oriented. Senior Inquiry faculty work to find out what students want to do in terms of their major interests and help students apply their disciplinary skills and knowledge to the community projects. Some courses are "by permission of instructor" because they need particular skills or aptitudes for the projects, (such as multimedia experience).

In the "Problems in Intercultural Communication" Senior Inquiry, the lead instructor collaborates with two writing instructors and community partners to promote intercultural communication. As outlined on the syllabus, the capstone objectives are to "identify and analyze politically constructed categories of race, age, class, and gender, in society against the backdrop of debates on multiculturalism in the U.S. The course examines these categorizations of race, class, etc. in their historical, political, social and cultural context and how those [categorizations] have influenced mass-mediated and interpersonal communication" (J. Patton, personal communication, April 2003).

Students write reflection papers in response to the assigned readings and relate issues raised in the readings to their experiences at the community sites. At their community sites, students take field notes based on their observations of social interactions and activities. The major assignment for the course is a research paper studying an intercultural communication problem that involves their immediate community (the community organization to which they are assigned). The written reports include a statement of the problem, the objectives of the study, a brief overview of previous research, and analysis and interpretation of data (personal interview(s) and field notes).

Promoting Information Literacy

Developing information literacy is another aim of the learning communities for engineering students at Drexel University. The engineering librarian, the information literacy librarian, the engineering faculty, and the program coordinators for the engineering design projects collaborate to incorporate information literacy components in each year of the engineering curriculum.

In the first year, students work in teams of about four students to complete a design project. Each team is assigned an engineering adviser and a humanities, technical writing adviser. In addition, engineering librarians work with the students on their design projects. At the beginning of the second quarter, the librarians conduct mandatory one-hour sessions in the library that focus on

(1) finding articles and other resources by using examples from engineering design projects and (2) understanding web versus database search strategies. Later in the quarter, each design team has an individual consultation with a librarian, either in person or via e-mail, to brainstorm and locate specific resources related to the teams' design project (J. Bhata, personal communication, April 2003).

In each phase of this instruction, careful attention has been paid to the many factors required for a highly effective program, including face-to-face and asynchronous learning opportunities, collaborative relationships between the library and the academic departments, assessments to measure student progress, tools to evaluate the success of the program, and a full complement of one-on-one and small group follow-up sessions to create a lasting relationship between the students, their research, and the information specialists and resources available through the library (V. Arms, personal communication, April 2003).

Librarians are members of the instructional teams that plan and present the first-year seminars that are included in many of the learning communities at Indiana University Purdue University Indianapolis. The IUPUI Template for First-Year Seminars (May 2002, http://www.universitycollege.iupui.edu/) outlines the intended learning outcomes for the course. Under the broader objective that "Students should understand the role and make full use of IUPUI resources and services which support their learning and campus connections," the template identifies the following objectives for library use and information retrieval:

> Distinguish between the open and invisible web (which includes library resources) and be able to use both in support of their academic work.
> Demonstrate the ability to find a book and an article pertaining to a specific information need or research assignment, using the library resources.
> Identify the major services provided by the university library and use the reference desk for further guidance [p. 7].

One IUPUI librarian developed two activities to help students explore the credibility of sources. In one exercise, students are given "scientific" articles from a variety of sources, including tabloid sources. In groups, students consider the science described in each article and discuss whether they think the information is credible. These group decisions are then reviewed with the rest of the class. "This provides a nice opportunity to discuss issues of credibility as well as the scientific method and acceptable evidence" (W. Orme, personal communication, April 2003).

In another lesson, students and their teachers explore definitions of "credible sources." Students are given an index card with the name of an information source. Two labels are pasted on the classroom wall: "credible" and "not credible." Students are asked to individually place their index cards somewhere between these two extremes. The librarian discusses students' placements and then the class is invited to come up and reassign any cards (sources) they think should be moved. The librarian then discusses the changes. Major changes are examined, and students who made the adjustments are asked to explain their reasons. Finally, the faculty member teaching the course is invited to make changes and explain his or her reasoning. The goal for this lesson is to help students begin to understand the gap between what they consider a credible source and what an academic professional considers a credible source. Students are also introduced to important library resources such as subscription databases.

Conclusion

Teachers and students in learning communities own the curriculum. Although curricular planning begins with the teachers, for students to become truly vested in learning, they must also feel ownership and responsibility for the curricular goals and intended outcomes. From beginning (coming together to discuss course goals) to middle (reflecting on how things are going and making small adjustments) to end (assessing curricular effectiveness and modifying goals and plans), teachers in learning communities should raise and revisit the central questions: What do we want students to know? What should students be able to do? Intentional planning, clearly articulated outcomes, and opportunities for students to engage in active learning centered around well-defined learning objectives are important characteristics of curricular learning communities. They are also the trademarks of a curriculum development process that moves students' experience in learning communities beyond the social value of taking courses with other students.

CHAPTER FOUR

PEDAGOGY THAT BUILDS COMMUNITY

Jodi Levine Laufgraben, Daniel Tompkins

College educators have been using "learning communities" of some sort for nearly a century. In many cases, the instructional mode has remained quite traditional, featuring a lecturer or team of lecturers and an emphasis on passive classroom learning. Even Joseph Tussman's Experimental College Program at the University of California, as chronicled by Katherine Bernhardi Trow (1998), seems not to have "experimented" very much with this instructional mode. Faculty expounded to audiences (pp. 90–97), and seminars were considered worthwhile, but "neither Tussman nor the other faculty were clear from the beginning about either the size of the seminars or just how they would work" (p. 98). Here and elsewhere, pedagogical improvement for a long time hinged on enhancement to a traditional system: better lectures, neater presentations, more attention to student questions.

The key development over the past two decades has been to take the "learning community" with a new sort of inquisitive seriousness by asking how *do* students learn best. A very influential stage in this development came, surprisingly, in the area of calculus teaching, again at the University of California. Trying to understand in the late 1980s why some students did better than others in a calculus course, Uri Treisman (1992) noticed that successful students studied in different ways, forming study groups to review material and reinforcing each others' learning. What was remarkable about this finding was that student learning had nothing to do with improved lecturing, better or more animated presentation by the teacher, or visual aids; it was a function of the social organization of students.

This is an example of college faculty inquiring how students learned best. The lecture and all other pedagogies and methods became subjects of study. The focus shifted from presentation to reception: still keenly aware of how we organize our classes and how we move onstage, teachers are becoming increasingly attentive to how students use information and build knowledge. Teaching and learning have become a paired set, organically linked, the systole and diastole of college education.

Effective Teaching

The first thing the literature says about "effective teaching" then is that teaching should be linked with learning. Teaching in the sense of a polished presentation is worthless if it does not affect student understanding. The past two decades have seen a surge of interest in how students learn.

Scholars of learning fall into no single camp. They come from different disciplines and have different goals. But a random walk through their work reveals a certain convergence: many of these scholars are interested in learning that is retained and influential; many are finding that both active learning and interactivity help promote this sort of long-term or deep learning.

Active Learning

A British team led by psychologist Martin A. Conway (1997) sought to determine the factors that bring about long-term understanding. A rigorous experiment found that remembered knowledge is a crucial building block of further learning, so crucial that the team coined a term: the "Remember to Know" or "R to K" shift. Active learning exercises that present knowledge in different contexts facilitate the schematization that turns data into knowledge (pp. 395–400). The authors do not go into great detail about the nature of active learning but do associate it with the presentation of knowledge in different contexts.

Clearly, all learning is somehow "active." As Theodore Marchese (1997) points out, "passive learning is an oxymoron" (p. 88). But what Marchese and others have in mind is a learning experience in which "knowing what, how, and why" provides a full understanding of a topic. Marchese is building in part on the work of Marton (1998) in Sweden and Entwhistle (1998) in Scotland, who distinguished "deep" from "surface" learning, deep learning being learning that has meaning for the student and that is retained.

Current literature on student learning is packed with references to "active learning," but the studies by Marton (1998) and Entwistle (1998) remain rewarding to read. In a passage full of import for learning communities, Marchese (1997) alludes to recent work by Entwistle that shows, "[A]nxiety, fear of failure, and low self-esteem are associated with surface approaches to learning. Further, students are more likely to engage in active forms of learning when they believe that their own effort, rather than external factors beyond their control, determines success" (p. 87). Marchese urges university faculty to build up students' sense of control over their work and to encourage them to exercise responsibility for their own learning.

Pedagogy That Builds Community

Pedagogy that builds community has several characteristics:

1. Acknowledges that students and teacher(s) share responsibility for learning
2. Helps students recognize the importance of learning from each other
3. Involves careful thinking about the nature and context of assignments
4. Emphasizes that learning is a process, not just an outcome

Pedagogy that builds community recognizes that learning and community are both a means and an end. Community is a strategy that strengthens learning, and in learning communities students learn to work and understand more deeply the value and challenges of community (MacGregor, 1996). Pedagogy that creates and enhances community is an approach to teaching and learning in which the student and faculty share responsibility for creating knowledge. Several pedagogical approaches that foster deeper learning and community are discussed in this chapter: (1) collaborative learning, (2) group assignments, (3) journals, (4) discussion, and (5) uses of technology. This is not an exhaustive list of active pedagogy. Service learning, experiential learning, undergraduate research programs, and problem-based learning are other approaches also found in learning communities programs and classrooms.

Collaborative Learning

A superior review of the achievements and potential of cooperative or collaborative learning in the college classroom is *Cooperative Learning for Higher Education Faculty* (Millis and Cottell, 1998). An introductory chapter reviews the "commonalities" between the cooperative and collaborative approaches:

- Learning is active.
- Students present ideas before others.
- Students take responsibility for their own learning.
- Teachers emphasize higher-order thinking.
- Teachers blend lecture and group work, stressing the development of team skills and working in diverse groups [pp. 6–7].

An example of collaborative learning in the college classroom is provided by Finkel (2000), who used the term "conceptual workshops" to refer to small in-class work groups in which students work on a particular problem or class. "This phrase emphasizes the conceptual nature of both the learning aimed for and the work required of the workshop's designer" (p. 96). The conceptual workshop can range from fifty minutes to as long as four hours, depending on the class's scheduled meeting time. The teacher(s) set the size of the group depending on the nature of the assigned task. Typically students gather into groups of four or so, work for a good amount of time on a worksheet, and then report the results of their work with the full class. Finkel recommends incorporating conceptual workshops into the routine of the class. "Students need to become accustomed to the different kinds of demands these classes make on them, to the different rhythm of work, and the different classroom atmosphere. They also need to get a taste of their distinct intellectual rewards" (p. 97).

The well-designed conceptual workshop should accomplish three objectives:

1. Convert a product of knowledge into a process.
2. Provide a whole experience with a beginning, middle, and end.
3. Get the teacher out of the middle of the classroom configuration [Finkel, 2000, p. 100].

The informal learning team is designed to reinforce instruction and help students make connections to prior course content and learning. Activities are narrower than with the formal teams, and team members engage in introductory or transitional exercises. The duration of these teams might be as brief as one class meeting. Small groups can be used to

- Generate ideas in preparation for a lecture, film, and so on
- Summarize main points in a text, reading, film, or lecture
- Assess levels of skills and understanding
- Reexamine ideas present in previous classes
- Review exams, problems, quizzes, and writing assignments
- Process learning outcomes at the end of class
- Provide comments to teachers on how a class is going
- Compare and contrast key theories, issues, and interpretations
- Solve problems that relate theory to practice
- Brainstorm applications of theory to everyday life [Meyers and Jones, cited at http://lsn.curtin.edu.au/learn_online/topics/wosmalgroup.html]

Richard Felder teaches chemical engineering at North Carolina State University and is widely respected as a teacher of engineering. In a report coauthored with Rebecca Brent, Felder (1994) stated: "Relative to students taught traditionally–i.e., with instructor-centered lectures, individual assignments, and competitive grading–cooperatively taught students tend to exhibit higher academic achievement, greater persistence through graduation, better high-level reasoning and critical thinking skills, deeper understanding of learned material, more on-task and less disruptive behavior in class, lower levels of anxiety and stress, greater intrinsic motivation to learn and achieve, greater ability to view situations from others' perspectives, more positive and supportive relationships with peers, more positive attitudes toward subject areas, and higher self-esteem" (http://www.ncsu.edu/felder-public/Papers/Coopreport.html).

Felder and Brent also noted, however, that their students groused and resisted when engaged in group exercises. "Instructors who don't anticipate a negative reaction . . . can easily get discouraged," they say. However, they add that at the end of the term, "The course evaluations were exceptionally high and most students made strong statements about how much the group work improved their understanding of the course material" (http://www.ncsu.edu/felder-public/Papers/Coopreport.html).

Felder and Brent (1994), master teachers in a well-supported program, regularly obtained "exceptionally high" evaluations but acknowledged "grousing." As learning communities and collaborative learning models expand, educators cannot expect that structures themselves will automatically bring progress. As in most forms of teaching, the personal warmth, depth of knowledge, and organizational skills of a teacher are likely to have as much influence as the structure that teacher adopts for classroom learning. Faculty recruitment and development, along with program assessment activities, must continue to focus on these pedagogical virtues. In collaborative settings, faculty understanding of student responses is particularly necessary: this method of teaching reminds some students of unproductive drills in secondary school and seems to others to remove the teacher's responsibility for learning. A good deal of skill is required in winning students over to the productive features of this learning model.

Group Assignments

In a learning community, uses of groups can range from informal small group activities in class to more formal in-class group work to group assignments requiring teamwork over the course of the term or semester. In linked-course or clustered communities, group projects can be assigned across courses in the community, with a portion of the project grade applied to each individual course.

Since the teachers in learning communities frequently rely on collaborative learning approaches, group projects or team assignments are commonly used in communities (Stein and Hurd, 2000). Group projects come with their own list of challenges. Most frequently occurring problems involve variability in group performance, both within and across groups, and decisions about grading (individual versus group grades). Group assignments need to be carefully designed and implemented if community is to be developed and cooperative learning realized. An activity designed to promote cooperative learning should have the following characteristics (Johnson and Johnson, 1999; Meyers and Jones, 1993; Stein and Hurd, 2000):

- A sense of interdependence among team members
- Accountability of individual students to both team and instructor
- Frequent face-to-face interaction to promote team goals
- Development of social skills needed for collaboration
- Critical analysis of group processes

Teams can take different shapes, but the configuration of student groups or teams should be closely aligned with the goals for the learning activity. The formal learning team is formed to teach specific content. Team activities are well planned, and the size, composition, and duration of the team are consistent with the instructional goals. Guidance and monitoring is ongoing, and the activity includes formal evaluation.

Students in a sociology learning community at Temple University engaged in a team project centered on the community theme, "Thinking Beyond the Self."

The team activity was designed and implemented in the freshman seminar, which was linked to a section of college composition and a larger sociology course. The activity was designed to enhance students' understanding of culture, a key concept for the sociology course. The structure of this group activity and many of the team-building activities and the assessments used in this project came from a summer faculty development workshop featuring Sandra Hurd, director of the Learning Communities program at Syracuse University and coauthor of the book, *Using Student Teams in the Classroom* (Stein and Hurd, 2000). Hurd provided resources to Temple faculty that are also available on the Temple Learning Communities website [http://www.temple.edu/university_studies/faculty_resources.html].

Each student team was required to research a particular aspect of college student culture. Students formed teams early in the semester. Before the teams even began work on the assignment, they participated in several team-building activities. First, each team had to come up with a name and logo. Then each team had to write a charter establishing rules governing group behavior (meeting times, absence policies, expectations for each group member's contribution to the final project). Teams also competed against each other in a campus scavenger hunt designed to promote teamwork.

Teams then engaged in web and library research on their topics. Some class time was allotted for group work, but most of their information gathering took place outside of class. Each team submitted a three- to five-page group paper and delivered a presentation to the class that included visual aids. Along the way, team members completed individual and group assessments.

Students in the Management Learning Community at Syracuse University enroll in three common courses: introduction to management, introduction to writing, and a learning community seminar. They also reside on a floor in a designated residence hall. Course projects, introduced in the management course, are central to the learning outcomes for the community. For example, one team conducted an analysis of the toy industry. A team of seven students produced a sixty-page report that included the history of the industry, its competitive structure, a marketing prospectus, and recommendations for strategic change [http://www.som.syr.edu/facstaff/snhurd/learning_community/courses2.html]. As described by the management professor: "The strong academic connection among Management Learning Community students and faculty creates very successful course projects" [http://www.som.syr.edu/facstaff/snhurd/learning_community/courses2.html].

Journals

Journals are commonly used in English or writing courses but are also assigned in courses with experiential learning or fieldwork components—nursing and education, for example—so students can document their professional growth and development. Journals may also be used in disciplines such as anthropology and sociology that frequently rely on learning through observation (Fulwiler, 1987). According to Fulwiler, "journals have become recognized useful pedagogical tools in other disciplines–not just English–where critical independent thought, speculation, or exploration is important" (p. 1). In addition to language features (colloquial dictation, pronoun and punctuation use, and rhythms of everyday speech), good journals are also characterized by several cognitive activities:

- Observations
- Questions
- Speculation
- Self-awareness
- Digression
- Synthesis
- Revision
- Information [p. 3]

In the learning community, journal writing is a useful activity to deepen learning and curricular integration. The journal assignment should be grounded in solid pedagogical reasoning, and the purposes of journals should be clear to students from the onset. According to Bruner as quoted in Fulwiler (1987): "When people articulate connections between new information and what they already know, they learn and understand that new information better" (p. 5). Writing about this new information furthers students' learning and understanding.

According to Fulwiler (1987), teachers can assign journals for a variety of reasons. First, journals help students make connections between what they study in class and read in the textbook(s). Second, journals can also be the place where students think about and process course content. Or third, a journal can be used to collect data, observations, and responses. A fourth use is to allow students to practice writing before formal assignments are submitted for grading.

In a first-year seminar, "Schools, Community, and Power," in the Michigan Community Scholars Program, students were required to interview a family member on their experiences in the 1960s and to compare their reflections to an assigned reading. Journal excerpts from the assignment were compiled and shared with students for in-class discussion. One student wrote:

> After reading Sugrue, I realized that my family's account of their experiences during that time period were not all that far fetched. I always considered my parents to be moderate in their beliefs. Liberal in some senses, such as accepting others, or being open to new and fresh ideas, but rather conservative in other areas especially when differentiating between right and wrong. As we

discussed the 60s and 70s and then got carried away and continued to discuss about more modern times, it became clear to me how different people could be in their viewpoints, especially after reading the excerpts drawn together in Robert Mast's book *Detroit Lives* [D. Schoem, personal communication, January 2002].

Through journals, students can reflect on the academic and social experiences of being members of a community. If students are required to complete a group or team project, a team journal can be assigned (Graybeal, 1987). A team journal can reside in a neutral location, perhaps on reserve at the library, or can be stored electronically on a course website. As described by Graybeal, students are required to make one entry per week in the team journal. The task is to read what another group member has written and to then share one's own thoughts and feelings on the topic. The teacher reads the entries weekly and provides a general response as to how the team is doing. "The general benefits I have observed include an increase in students' appropriation and integration of course material, development of personal interest and investment in the topic, independent wondering and questioning and connecting, and even the improvement of writing skills, especially fluidity and ease of expression" (p. 307).

Ellen Hernandez uses a community journal in her learning community at Camden County College to promote teacher-student and peer-peer communication among students. The journal circulates during class meetings and is returned to Professor Hernandez at the end of class. Students' entries range from current events to personal frustrations to grading concerns to classroom management issues. The professor gets the writing started with a prompt, such as: "I hear some people talking about various frustrations in class, in school, work, life. I know being a student can be very frustrating. I imagine some of you are frustrated even about your grade on your first writing assignment in this class. Will you share some of those frustrations here in this journal?" (E. Hernandez, personal communication, January 2002).

Students can use the journal to express their feelings, thereby cluing the teacher in to personal or academic problems that might be affecting their performance in the course. In response to the above prompt, one student shared his personal connection to America's war on terrorism: "I am also frustrated with this terrorist attack on us because I have a brother in the Air Force right now and he is stationed in Korea. He was supposed to be home for Thanksgiving, but after this, I don't even know if he'll be home for Christmas. And I'm frustrated because I want more than anything for him to be safe. Do you think this qualifies for frustration?"

At another point in the semester, Professor Hernandez used the journals to probe students' feelings about their course portfolio. After praising their efforts, she asked whether any students had comments about the process of creating the portfolio. One student wrote: "I had no idea how to do a portfolio, so I used the examples from the book as a guide. But I also wanted to do my own work, so I worked on it as hard as I could. I hope I did well. I like getting good grades on my own for once."

Discussion

In their book *Discussion as a Way of Teaching,* Stephen D. Brookfield and Stephen Preskill (1999) list fifteen benefits of discussion:

1. It helps students explore a diversity of perspectives.
2. It increases students' awareness of and tolerance for ambiguity or complexity.
3. It helps students recognize and investigate their assumptions.
4. It encourages attentive, respectful listening.
5. It develops new appreciation for continuing differences.
6. It increases intellectual agility.
7. It helps students become connected to a topic.
8. It shows respect for students' voices and experiences.
9. It helps students learn the process and habits of democratic discourse.
10. It affirms students as co-creators of knowledge.
11. It develops the capacity for the clear communication of ideas and meaning.
12. It develops habits of collaborative learning.
13. It increases breadth and makes students more empathic.
14. It helps students develop skills of synthesis and integration.
15. It leads to transformation [pp. 22–23].

Of particular interest to learning communities, discussion can help students learn the process of democratic discourse, emphasize students' roles as co-creators of knowledge, promote collaborative learning, and enhance the skills of synthesis and integration.

By definition, learning in community promotes democratic discourse. Through discussions, students can practice the skills and habits of democratic discourse—respecting diverse perspectives, accepting decisions that represent opposing viewpoints, and recognizing instances when at best there is only a partial execution of democratic principles.

Discussions are a good way to step down from "the sage on the stage role" and transfer responsibility for making meaning to the students, as both individuals and a community of learners. According to Brookfield and Preskill (1999), if students come to realize that their views and knowledge are respected and that they are considered co-creators of knowledge, they will take discussion more seriously. Students should feel that their contributions to the community's discussion are invaluable.

Discussion as pedagogy promotes collaborative learning. Learning to listen is an important skill of discussion and collaboration, as is learning to value the contributions of others to the conversation. It is important to emphasize the importance of collaboration and respect in discussion so that students will practice these skills in informal discussion settings, such as conversations over meals, discussions in study groups, and on-line chats.

In linked courses, teachers can use discussion to build on topics discussed in the other course in the community. By beginning class with the simple prompt, "What did you talk about in sociology today?" a discussion emerges that helps students discover the curricular connections around which the community is built. Discussion helps students probe commonalities between courses. When students make these connections on their own, their learning deepens.

Not all discussion need occur in the classroom. Listservs, course websites, and e-mail exchanges also promote continued discussions outside of formal class meetings. For the more reserved student, electronic discussions might offer a more private, less intimidating place to share thoughts and perspectives. E-dialogue is also an opportunity for students to exchange ideas publicly while they privately work through readings and assignments.

Technology

Technology can be used to combine journal writing and discussion. In the reflective tutorial section in the "Sense and Nonsense in Science" learning community at Wagner College, students participate in a journal webboard. The goal of the reflective tutorial is the integration of study in biology and psychology with students' experiences in their community field placement. Reading, writing, and discussion are used to promote development of students' communication and analytic skills (course website, http://www.wagner.edu/faculty/users/lnolan/rft/rft2001.htm). Students are required to make two postings per week to the webboard and are graded on both their entries to the on-line journal and their responses to other students' postings. Suggested topics include

- Reflections on your first days at Wagner.
- Reflections on your first days in class. Is college what you thought it would be?

- Your first impressions of your classes.
- Reflections on your reading assignments. What are you learning on your own? In class?
- Reflections on the process by which you chose your experiential placement.

> What do you hope to learn there?
> What goals will you set for yourself in this experience?
> What were your initial impressions of the agencies at the open house?
> What decision did you make?

- Reflect on your first visit to the agency.

> How did you get there?
> What is the setting like?
> Who are the people you met and what are your initial impressions?

- Report and reflect on various aspects of the placement experience (see attached page).
- Reflect on the connections between the courses in your LC (psychology and biology). Explore the connections between them and your placement (this may not always be obvious—there may be many more subtle interconnections).
- Compare your other courses with the LC courses. Have you learned some unexpected connections there?
- As the semester approaches midterm and finals, reflect back on your previous postings.

> How have your expectations been met?
> How have they not been met?
> Describe some unexpected experiences/benefits you have discovered.
> (course website, http://www.wagner.edu/faculty/users/lnolan/rft/journal.htm).

Students can use the webboard to discuss readings and key concepts. They respond to each others' postings, and the teacher can use the on-line discussions to raise further questions for discussion or to challenge students to clarify their thoughts. Exhibit 4.1 illustrates a webboard discussion between the teacher and a student on the topics of "the mind-body problem" and interactionism.

EXHIBIT 4.1. EXAMPLE OF AN ON-LINE DISCUSSION

Conf: History of Psychology (LC)
From: STUDENT
Date: Tuesday, February 05, 2002 09:23 P.M.

I agree with the identity theory of materialism; I still believe in God though. I think the soul is separate from consciousness; it gives us the energy to live and think. The soul activates consciousness in the brain and the physical functions in the body. After much debate, I am pretty sure I think the mind and brain are one, there are just separate perceptions to be interpreted—objective body and subjective mind. The soul is from the spiritual world, not consciousness.

Topic: Mind-body problem (2 of 4), Read 10 times
Conf: History of Psychology (LC)
From: TEACHER
Date: Tuesday, February 05, 2002 10:38 P.M.

It sounds like you're describing interactionism: "soul activates consciousness." Care to clarify?

Topic: Mind-body problem (3 of 4), Read 8 times
Conf: History of Psychology (LC)
From: STUDENT
Date: Sunday, February 10, 2002 08:40 P.M.

I guess that is what I described. I do think that the soul activates the mind, but I don't think the mind is consciousness. Consciousness is more of awareness I think. But we already discussed that in class. I think once a soul enters a body, a mind is formed and becomes gradually complex through experience. Like a child is born with a very simple mind and it grows as the child grows. I hope I don't sound crazy!

Topic: Mind-body problem (4 of 4), Read 8 times
Conf: History of Psychology (LC)
From: TEACHER
Date: Monday, February 11, 2002 08:18 A.M.

I will be honest with you—because of these complexities, I rejected the one thing for which there is no scientific evidence: the soul. No one asked me, but I thought I would let you know what I think since you have all shared your thoughts.

At Temple, teachers rely on Blackboard—a web-based, course management tool—to supplement in-class instruction and to encourage intellectual interactions beyond instructional time. Blackboard has several communication tools that can facilitate discussions. A discussion board can be used for threaded dialogue on course topics. The groups feature can allow designated groups to post discussions on team projects or topics of interest. There is also an e-mail feature that allows the instructor or other students to send e-mails to the entire class or selected course users. In a criminal justice learning community at Temple, the criminal justice professor uses Blackboard to facilitate dialogue among student groups:

> One thing it did facilitate, and which was done specifically for the LC component of the course, was to allow me to set up groups on the account. In the class there was a group project and by setting up groups on the account I was able to talk directly to each member of the group, allow members to e-mail each other easily (like a mini-listserve for the group) and use the group-based discussion board. This group feature did improve the ability of the group to communicate with each other in the development of their paper and presentation. It also allowed them to become familiar and comfortable with the technology of Blackboard (P. Jones, personal communication, December 2001).

In Chandler-Gilbert Community College's "Teachers Today and Tomorrow" (T3) learning community, a computer information sciences course (Internet II) is linked with first-year composition and Introduction to Education. Students are introduced to a variety of software programs (Microsoft FrontPage, Internet Explorer, Microsoft Office) that will allow them to "connect to an even larger community for research, communication, and presentation" (B. Mullaney, personal communication, December 2001).

The T3 Blackboard site houses useful information that students can access at any time. The site includes information about the course and the teachers, including contact information and photos. Under "resources" students find links to websites related to the teaching profession and a link to an on-line writing lab that provides grammar and writing assistance. The teachers in this community also use the Blackboard site to post sample teaching portfolios. From the Blackboard site, students can access up to ten teaching portfolios compiled by education majors at colleges and universities across the country.

Although many learning community teachers praise approaches that promote community and active learning, others voice frustrations. "You can't cover as much content. It's a whole different game assessing learning when it occurs in collective contexts. Journals take inordinate amounts of time to grade or otherwise respond to" (M. Weimer, personal communication, July 2003). Faculty development, discussed in the next chapter, is essential to ensuring good teaching practice in learning communities. Faculty development brings teachers together to talk about the challenges, successes, and failures of using collaborative or active forms of pedagogy or technology in their classrooms.

The Challenges of Teaching with Others

The pedagogical approaches described in this chapter may involve a different type of teaching for some faculty members. As described by Jean MacGregor (2000), in learning communities, teams of individuals need to sail a single vessel. "For a sustained period of time—a quarter or a semester or even a year—teaching teams commit themselves to a course or program with a common group of students. Sailing together requires teamwork, collaborative skills, and collective responsibility that are less familiar to those of us in the habit of sailing solo" (http://learningcommons.evergreen.edu/pdf/spring2000b.pdf, p. 1).

Teaching in a learning community requires faculty members to change how they teach. "The first step in interdisciplinary collaboration, whether in teaching or research, is accepting the different practices and beliefs of others" (Cornwell and Stoddard, 2001, p. 162). Teaching is no longer an isolated activity but rather a community commitment. By design, learning communities promote transformations. In addition to transforming courses to programs and disciplinary perspectives to interdisciplinary contexts, good pedagogy in learning communities requires moving from teaching alone to teaching with others. Team teaching requires team building, collaborative skills, and collective responsibility.

Team Building and Teamwork

Faculty development activities should include discussion and activities that promote positive teamwork. The biggest challenge is time—finding time to bring already busy people together to function as a team. Sustaining teamwork is also a challenge. Commitments to the learning community are challenged when other realities set in. "Our individual units and home departments continuously reel us back in. Our competitive and individualistic training has often not prepared us for the public nature and give-and-take of collaborative teaching" (MacGregor, 2000, p. 2). Some strategies for promoting teamwork across learning communities teaching teams include

- Clearly articulate expectations for the teaching team.
- Recognize and reward planning efforts (planning lunches for teachers, stipends for summer planning time, professional development funds for travel to conferences).

- Be flexible when scheduling team planning events (a one-shot deal workshop only works if all members of a team can be present). Set aside several dates and times for planning sessions and require teaching teams to participate as a group.
- Provide examples of successful teamwork in learning communities.
- Avoid (whenever possible) changes in teaching assignments once a team has formed and started its work.
- Suggest that teaching teams set meeting schedules well in advance, particularly days and times to meet once the semester begins.
- Create or suggest space where teaching teams can meet. Space that is away from individual offices or departments may allow for more focused, less interrupted team planning time.

Collaborative Skills

In addition to teamwork, teaching in a learning community requires important social skills, including trust, mutual understanding, communication, and conflict management. Traditionally, teaching is a private activity; in learning communities, it is public. Individuals need to share information about their courses and teaching with others in their program or community. A supportive context for discussing teaching and providing feedback is important to collaboration. Each team member must take care and responsibility for building and respecting this context.

Collective Responsibility

The success of the learning community depends on students' and teachers' experiences across the community and not just in one or the other course. From presemester planning to reinforcement of the curricular theme to assessing student learning, teaching in learning communities is a collective responsibility. At the program level, faculty development and teacher materials should outline the expectations for teaching teams; individual teaching teams should then reach consensus on shared responsibilities for community planning, assignments, class activities, assessment, and so on.

Faculty in learning communities share responsibility for becoming a teaching team. Problems arise when a teaching teams fails to gel. This may happen for a variety of reasons: varied levels of interest in the goals and expectations for learning communities, different teaching and learning styles, conflicting priorities, competing schedules. Level of commitment is another potential problem. After strong initial interest, one or some members of a teaching team may fail to carry their load or may stop attending planning meetings. Once the semester gets under way, faculty are busy with course management, department obligations, and off-campus commitments. "The best-laid plans. . ." becomes a reality, and the full potential for the learning community may not be realized. Program leadership plays an important role in helping teaching teams come together and stay on task. Schedule opportunities for all learning community faculty to come together to share successes and frustrations, be a facilitator to help teams stay focused and functioning, acknowledge up front that problems arise, and offer steps that other teaching teams took to move beyond barriers and function as a team.

Teachers in learning communities also have a collective responsibility to articulate the community or program theme. Do not assume that students are as aware of the curricular theme as you believe. Constant references to the theme will reinforce expectations for deeper learning and curricular integration. Communicate often with teaching partners. Share "hits" as well as "misses" in terms of instructional goals. Talk about student performance and ways to improve the community. Ask, How are we doing as a community of teachers? For faculty, regardless of the model of learning community, satisfaction with the learning communities teaching experience often depends on the shared responsibility for the curriculum, teaching, and learning. According to one experienced learning communities teacher: "For me, the satisfaction comes from the degree of integration and collaboration, no matter which of the two models I'm teaching in" (L. Dunlap, personal communication, September 2002).

In addition to the interpersonal challenges, those teaching in learning communities may encounter structural barriers to forming and participating on teaching teams. Systems for calculating workloads, release time, and rewards may not recognize or properly value team teaching. Conflicts may arise between the goals for learning communities and department objectives or institutional priorities. A department may discourage junior faculty members from teaching in learning communities to allow professors on the tenure track time for research and scholarship. A college or university may consider teaching a one-credit seminar linked to a learning community as voluntary overload. However, when teachers come together to teach in learning communities and the program steadily expands across campus, there is tremendous potential for change. Additional challenges, strategies, and benefits specific to teaching in the different models of learning communities are described in the next sections.

Freshman Interest Groups (FIGs)

Resources for faculty development, preparation time for faculty, and lack of faculty interest are obstacles faced by FIG programs (Learning Communities Directory, National Learning Communities Project, http://learningcommons.

evergreen.edu/06_directory_entry.asp). Another challenge, one faced across models, is a lack of interdisciplinary teaching experience among faculty.

In FIGs, some classes will have mixed enrollments of FIG and non-FIG students. Expectations for teacher communication will vary from program to program. When teachers are not fully aware of the FIG group or the theme around which the courses in the FIG are organized, this can be problematic: "I had put together a course on cultural contact in short fiction by contemporary British and American writers. Then I was assigned the 'Heavens' FIG: mythology and astronomy. Some students faulted me on evaluations because the course did not relate to their FIG. Basically if there's any way to let instructors know sooner what FIG they will have, perhaps they could have time to plan course content accordingly" (Lowell, 1997, p. 19).

When FIG teachers do communicate with each other, they find it useful, particularly the chance to meet with FIG leaders or students to discuss student progress and concerns. "One group sent me a thank-you card after I met with them and their FIG leader. That was a very pleasant surprise. Some of the FIG students were the best students in the class in terms of asking questions during lecture" (Lowell, 1997, p. 18).

In terms of changes to their teaching when their courses are part of FIGs, some professors find discussions are livelier and that it is easier to use small group work in class when FIG students are present. In a class composed primarily of freshmen, however, some teachers move more slowly in coverage of material or take time from content to explain policies and address how college is different from high school.

Norma Wilkerson, a faculty member at the University of Wyoming, has changed her teaching since teaching in FIGs. She teaches in a FIG that includes a University Studies course, psychology, and biology. "I try to make time for students out of class to increase learning activities. For example, I have organized a field trip to the Snowy Range for these students and I would not have done this in the past. I also try to provide students with opportunities to study together and plan for accomplishing group projects in their common courses. I find myself more of a facilitator of learning opportunities than a giver of knowledge" (personal communication, July 2002).

Collaborating with her other teachers remains a challenge. "I am currently trying to figure out ways to get the four instructors to interact more with students in the residence halls and to solicit student feedback relative to ways faculty can facilitate their active learning through community interaction."

The University of Washington addresses faculty development in its FIG program by convening a discussion group of teachers whose large lecture courses are dedicated to FIGs. The teachers meet regularly to discuss what is going on in their courses. This involves about ten faculty members whose FIG course enrollments represent about three thousand students (J. Johnson, personal communication, May 2002).

Linked or Clustered Courses

It is often assumed that teaching in a linked- or clustered-course learning community is less involved than teaching in a team-taught or coordinated studies program. Faculty members teaching in a linked- or clustered-course learning community teach discrete courses but work as a teaching team to integrate curriculum across the courses in the community. This requires a great deal of pre-semester and in-semester planning. The individual teachers need to come together early in the process to discuss their courses.

Presemester planning is important; once the semester begins, the individual teachers are likely to be pulled in many directions. Even the best-intentioned faculty struggle to find time for team planning once the regular demands of the semester (department meetings, committees, advising, teaching, and grading) start. If not all teachers participate in the planning conversations, the ability to create a community theme and plan around which teachers can build their individual courses is compromised.

Another planning challenge is determining how much integration or to what extent the courses should be aligned. Expectations for curricular integration need to be articulated and disseminated at the program level. The more difficult task of accomplishing that integration happens at the individual learning community level: "The biggest challenge for motivated teachers in linked classes is finding and articulating to students the links between the classes. Just presenting the same material from different angles doesn't work for most classes. No matter how fascinated scholars are by the different approaches to a subject, most students are aiming for understanding first, and so they miss or ignore the shadings of approach. On the other hand, if there is no overt overlap, the [learning community] can become only social" (A. Castaldo, personal communication, April 2002).

Interdisciplinary or Coordinated Studies Programs

Team-taught or coordinated studies models are the most intensive in terms of curricular integration and faculty collaboration. One challenge of teaching in coordinated studies involves coming together with colleagues to shape how learning outcomes will be met and how the different disciplinary perspectives can share teaching and learning space. Lynn Dunlap of Skagit Valley College describes challenges she has faced: "The challenges of coordinated studies for me have been in the willingness of colleagues to step back and revision how the learning outcomes are met. A few faculty who have been effective lecturers and have polished their courses into little gems of delivery haven't always understood (despite lots of conversations) how students could learn another way. In these courses we did provide integration and the students loved the course, but sometimes I felt that my course (usually film) was the place of intersection" (personal communication, September 2002).

There is tremendous potential for rewards. Adds Dunlap, "It's not often in a community college that you see young adults walking around with copies of William James' *Varieties of Religious Experience* in their coat pockets. It's not possible to get this kind of depth and complexity in a solo class, with its constraints of time and single discipline perspective" (personal communication, September 2002).

The Integrative Studies B.A./B.S. Program offered by New Century College at George Mason University consists of a general education learning community core, specializations in interdisciplinary subjects, and an experiential learning component (Oates, 2003). Freshmen enroll in four, eight-credit integrated learning communities (learning community units) team taught by faculty from various disciplines. The community meets over six to seven weeks for up to five hours a day. The challenge for the teacher is letting go of the autonomy characteristic of the traditional classroom to partner with others to create an experience for students that allows for deeper in-depth study and builds on previous course content. According to Janette Muir, associate dean for New Century College: "It is easy to walk into a classroom that you have full control over, where you don't have to deal with issues of accountability and challenges to academic rigor. It is much more difficult to collaborate with a colleague (or a team) to create a unique learning experience that will resonate for students and faculty alike. However, the synergy that is created from this kind of experience, through the intellectual exchange of ideas and healthy debate, greatly outweighs the loss of personal classroom autonomy and control" (personal communication, October 2003).

Achieving integration across the four community units is also a challenge. "In the case of a team-taught learning community the whole is often far greater than the sum of its parts. It can truly be a valuable integrative learning experience, where faculty can grow as much or even more than students" (personal communication, October 2003).

Residential Learning Communities

Residential learning communities or living-learning programs, discussed fully by David Schoem in Chapter Eight, offer tremendous promise for creating intellectual and social communities on campus. They also present, however, some unique challenges for faculty, student affairs administration, and residence life staff—all who play important roles in the creation and maintenance of these communities. Students may become more cliquish because they live together. Students may also perceive a class to be less important or more informal when it meets in the residence hall as opposed to a classroom building. Department colleagues may feel a faculty member is doing less work because he or she spends more time in the residence halls than around the department.

Teaching in a residential learning community also presents additional challenges in terms of logistics. Faculty are used to teaching in close to their offices, and teaching in a residence hall may mean a long walk, a drive, or a shuttle excursion to a classroom located in a residence hall. In addition, classrooms or faculty offices in residence halls may not be equipped with technological staples such as voice mail, e-mail, wipe boards, and soundproofing. Lack of parking, not enough chalk or chalkboard space, students bonding together to complain about a teacher are all reasons a faculty member may decide not to return to a residential learning community.

Teaching in a residential learning community requires planning for students' intellectual and social development. At St. Lawrence University, the first-year program is a living-learning program featuring an academic curriculum that begins with a team-taught multidisciplinary course that new students take in the fall. The teaching team consists of three faculty: someone from the natural sciences, someone from the social sciences, and a third person from the arts or humanities that share common, thematic interests. "Ideally, they also find one another's company sufficiently delightful that they can imagine spending the hours, the years, together that it takes to create and implement a successful First-Year Program college" (Cornwell and Stoddard, 2001, p. 165).

The program revolves around five clearly articulated goals:

Statement of Goals
Faculty, residential staff, and students will work together to

- Promote the integration of the academic and residential experience
- Encourage students to move toward patterns of living together that reflect principles of mutuality and accountability
- Encourage students to understand their rights and responsibilities as individuals residing in living-learning communities; for example, we will work

together to develop communities in which each student has enough quiet time to study and sleep enough to succeed as a student by helping residents understand their rights and responsibilities in relation to quiet hours and courtesy hours

- Help students make use of residential staff and faculty in exercising their rights and responsibilities while they develop the capacity for self-management
- Identify and confront conflicts before they become destructive of the living-learning community [http://web.stlawu.edu/fyp/resphilos.htm]

According to Cornwell and Stoddard (2001), these goals present some unique challenges for faculty teaching in a living-learning program. Faculty must pay close attention to the development of the whole student. This requires paying attention to students as individuals and to the community. Faculty frequently find themselves addressing issues of gender, substance abuse, or racism. "It is quite different to confront these issues in lived experience, with all of their immediacy, urgency, and reality, than through texts and data" (p. 168).

Conclusion

Pedagogy that builds community involves more than a toolbox of active approaches to teaching and learning. It also requires the skills of collaboration, respect, and trust. Faculty who teach in learning communities approach teaching as a craft and collectively with their colleagues experiment with new modes of pedagogy—such as collaborative learning, journal writing, and discussions—to engage their students. There are challenges, however, to teaching in new and more collaborative ways, challenges that should be addressed through ongoing dialogue with teachers, structural changes to how faculty work is rewarded, and assessment that demonstrates the impact of what happens when students learn in and from communities.

Teachers who are most engaged in the learning communities describe not only student learning but also their own learning and feelings of community. Returning to the sailing metaphor used by Jean MacGregor (2000) to describe teaching in learning communities and what faculty experience when they work collaboratively: "They [faculty] speak of the intense stimulation of discovering each others' disciplines and teaching practices, the affirmation of reflecting together on students they had in common, and the deep satisfaction of learning to collaboratively create a curriculum. They reflect on newfound trust and respect for their colleagues. In short, they loved being in the same boat" (p. 9).

CHAPTER FIVE

FACULTY DEVELOPMENT

Creating, improving, and sustaining learning communities requires ongoing attention to developing and supporting those who teach in learning communities. Faculty development involves "enhancing the talents, expanding the interests, improving the competence, and otherwise facilitating the professional and personal growth of faculty members, particularly in their roles as instructors" (Gaff, 1975, p. 14). Faculty development also refers to programs that focus on the individual faculty member as a teacher, scholar and professional, and person (Professional and Organizational Development Network in Higher Education, http://www.podnetwork.org/development/definitions.htm). Faculty development is central to the teaching and learning mission of learning communities and focuses not only on the teacher but also the curriculum. Instructional development–programs that focus on the "course, curriculum, and student learning" (Professional and Organizational Development Network in Higher Education, http://www.podnetwork.org/development/definitions.htm)–is also an important component in nurturing curricular learning communities.

Faculty development for learning communities seeks to create what the scholarship of teaching and learning literature describes as "communities of scholars" (Cambridge, 2001). In these communities, "faculty members study the ways in which they teach and students learn in their disciplines, and how campuses foster this scholarship at an institutional level" (p. 3). When faculty teaching in learning communities come together they also study how teachers teach and students learn *across* disciplines.

According to Hutchings (2000), this shift to a "culture of teaching and learning" (p. 1) invites teachers to explore a broader set of issues:

1. How teachers think and make decisions about method
2. The degree to which we share frameworks and goals for doing so
3. How we exchange with colleagues what we know and do as teachers
4. Whether and how our knowledge and practice are made public in ways that can be built up [p. 1]

Exploring teaching and student learning with colleagues is an important characteristic of the orientation and ongoing development of faculty teaching in learning communities.

Faculty development for learning communities creates the type of community of scholars that Cambridge (2001) describes. Cox (2001) describes faculty learning communities as empowering faculty to serve as change agents to move campuses from institutions to learning organizations. Building on the definition of student learning communities, faculty learning communities "build communication across disciplines, increase faculty interest in teaching and learning, initiate excursions into the scholarship of teaching, and foster civic responsibility" (p. 69). Faculty development is the road map to help teachers navigate the shift from the traditional ways of teaching to the more active and collaborative modes of pedagogy characteristic of learning communities.

Faculty Development for Learning Communities

Faculty development for learning communities has multiple purposes. Depending on the learning community model, faculty development might focus on the individual teacher as well as the teaching team. Instructional development might concentrate on the discretely taught courses or courses integrated to create a curriculum or program. On some campuses, faculty development is provided in collaboration with an established teaching and learning center. On most campuses, however, faculty and instructional development is the responsibility of program leadership, and learning community leaders and teachers are asked to wear the hat of educational developer. According to the Professional and Organizational Development Network in Higher Education (POD), "educational developers have a unique opportunity and a special responsibility to contribute to the quality of teaching and learning in higher education (Professional and Organizational Development Network in Higher Education, http://www.podnetwork. org/development/ethicalguidelines.htm).

Emerging models of teaching and learning in higher education, like learning communities, require new thinking about faculty roles, educational settings, and faculty development. "Such major and widespread institutional reform of faculty roles and student learning will not be successful without major efforts to provide faculty with the necessary skills, training, technology and support to perform these new roles" (Lieberman and Guskin, 2003, p. 261). Faculty development needs to be designed to help teachers in learning communities understand these shifts in instructional roles and classroom settings. Lieberman and Guskin identify several questions to consider when planning faculty development to support new higher education models:

1. How are faculty supported as they explore multiple pedagogical needs?
2. How are faculty supported as they deal with the new learning environments of the new models of higher education?
3. How are faculty supported as they expand their definitions and forms of scholarship?
4. How are individuals educated to evaluate faculty involved in new instructional roles and expanded forms of scholarship?
5. How are part-time and adjunct faculty assisted in their teaching roles at the institution?
6. How are faculty, staff, and students supported as they partner with members of the surrounding and international communities, as well as diversifying and internationalizing? [pp. 263–264]

In addition to these questions, it is important to consider who participates in faculty development for learning communities. Many faculty teaching in learning communities do so because they are already innovative, good teachers and they are already part of existing teaching and learning communities in their disciplines or departments. Many faculty teaching in learning communities possess knowledge and skills in the teaching methods often discussed at faculty development events for learning communities. These individuals should be included in the planning and delivery of faculty development events and should also be given opportunities to further practice and hone their craft with the teachers and students in their learning communities.

Faculty Development Activities

Faculty development programming can be divided into three sets of topics: (1) introduction to learning communities, (2) curricular planning and pedagogy, and (3) assessment and reflection. Exhibit 5.1 outlines some topics for each category.

EXHIBIT 5.1. FACULTY DEVELOPMENT TOPICS

Introduction to Learning Communities

1. Introduction of learning community models and definitions
2. Expectations for faculty
3. General dialogue on good practice in teaching and learning

Curricular Planning and Pedagogy

4. Conversations about curricular design and planning
5. Discussion of innovative pedagogies particularly appropriate to learning community settings
6. Dialogue about ways to build and foster community
7. Curriculum planning among teachers in a community

Assessment and Reflection

8. Discussion of assessment strategies suited for learning environments characterized by interdisciplinary study and collaborative learning
9. Time for reflection
10. Discussion of outcomes and plans for improvement

Introduction to Learning Communities

This topic is particularly important for new learning communities programs in the early stages of implementation or for programs that annually involve faculty who will be teaching in a learning community for the first time. Orientation should begin with a basic overview of the definitions and models of learning communities. There are multiple definitions of learning communities. (Definitions and models are reviewed in Chapter One.) It is important that a campus reach a mutual understanding of the definition that will guide their work and the model on which their communities will be based. If an institution offers linked-course learning communities, the faculty teaching in these communities should have a good understanding of the aims of this model. What are the strengths of this model? What are the particular challenges? What are the expectations for curricular integration? How will student learning be assessed across the courses in the community?

A PowerPoint presentation with handouts is a typical and efficient approach for addressing the nuts and bolts of goals, models, and definitions of learning communities, but faculty development should model the types of collaborative and interdisciplinary settings learning communities seek to create for students. It should be learner-centered, active, and collaborative. It should move away from lectures and presentations to include opportunities for group work and discussion. Instead of a presentation, faculty might discuss the goals of learning communities in small groups or work with colleagues from other disciplines to "design a learning community in an hour" (http://www.evergreen.edu/washcenter/LCHour.shtm).

Introduce the literature that supports the rationale for learning communities. Discuss research on how college affects students. Engage faculty in a discussion of the factors influencing student learning and student development both in and out of the classroom. In *Making the Most of College*, Light (2001) summarizes years of conversations with students about what made a difference in their college experience. Students want faculty and administrators who actively "get in their way" by offering opportunities, challenges, and guidance. They learn more by studying in groups and positively value racial and ethnic diversity. Teachers in learning communities can help students maximize their college experience by organizing them into out-of-class study groups, by having students share work through presentations, and by giving regular assessments that check for understanding of material.

Address faculty roles early in faculty development activities. Outline the expectations for faculty teaching in learning communities on your campus. Clarify expectations for participation in presemester and academic-year faculty development events. Inform teachers of available resources. Review any stipend, release time, or other rewards available for faculty teaching in communities and the conditions for receiving these rewards. Set guidelines for team planning. How often are teaching teams asked to meet? How often will they meet with program leadership? Expectations should be communicated early and can also be made available on a program website or in a faculty handbook. Temple University publishes roles for faculty along with presemester and semester planning guidelines in its faculty handbook (http://www.temple.edu/lc/faculty_resources.html).

Curricular Planning and Pedagogy

In this phase, faculty development moves from information gathering to curricular planning. The goal is to equip faculty with the tools and resources they need to successfully teach in a learning community setting. Conversations about curricular planning begin with the discussion of the learning community theme. What is the theme for this community, and how will our courses or disciplines come together around this theme?

Another important topic is the expectations for curricular integration dictated by the model. (Curriculum is discussed in Chapter Three.) Is the goal integrated or interdisciplinary curriculum? What are the intended outcomes for students? Faculty should be given time to discuss the curricular goals of their discipline and individual courses. A useful tool to stimulate this conversation is the Teaching Goals Inventory (TGI) from Angelo and Cross (1993).

The TGI is a short instrument that allows faculty to self-assess instructional goals for a particular course. The TGI features a list of possible teaching and learning goals, such as "Learn to understand perspectives and values of this subject" and "Develop analytical skills." Individuals are also asked to identify their primary role as a teacher. Responses are scored according to six clusters: (1) higher-order thinking skills, (2) basic academic success skills, (3) discipline-specific knowledge, (4) liberal arts and academic values, (5) work and career preparation, and (6) personal development.

Faculty can use results from their individually scored TGI to move to conversations about goals for the community. What were the commonalities or significant differences in terms of the goals rated "essential," "very important," or "unimportant"? How did each teacher in the learning community identify their primary role as a teacher? Faculty can facilitate curricular design and planning by discussing the similarities and differences in their teaching and learning goals.

From this point, the dialogue shifts to brainstorming about common readings, shared assignments, lectures, seminar topics, and out-of-class activities. Instructional development, particularly the learning community curriculum, becomes the focus. Within each course or discipline in the community, how will course content and pedagogy be connected to the learning community theme? Teaching methods are also discussed. Learning communities invite an array of pedagogical approaches that promote integrated or interdisciplinary teaching and learning (MacGregor, Smith, Matthews, and Gabelnick, 2002):

- Collaborative or cooperative learning
- Problem-based learning
- Teaching with case studies
- Lectures
- Demonstrations or labs
- Experiential learning
- Service learning
- Writing across the curriculum

Several of these approaches are described in Chapter Four. Faculty development activities should include an introduction to these promising ways of teaching and should provide ample opportunity for faculty to model and practice new techniques. When designing faculty development events, practice what you preach. Avoid lecturing to faculty about the virtues of more collaborative, learner-centered methods. If you want to promote collaborative learning in learning communities classrooms, faculty development activities should be characterized by small group activities and opportunities for faculty to exchange ideas and learn from each other.

During faculty development events, discuss strategies for building and fostering community among students and their teachers. Clearly articulate the expectations for members of this community. What does it mean to be part of *this* learning community? Talk about activities early in the semester—film showings, campus walks, community service projects—that promote community and build expectations for students as teams of learners. Ask participants to brainstorm approaches for extending academic conversations beyond the classroom. Ideas include listservs, journals, on-line discussion boards, study groups, and in-person or virtual chat sessions. Community building also involves shared responsibility for planning and reflecting on the activities of the community. Consider a mid-semester debriefing or survey to ask students how things are going and what they are experiencing in the community. What would they change? What topics or central themes are they having difficulty understanding or would they like to learn more about?

Faculty development activities should be structured so members of the community can plan and talk with each other. Ask faculty to bring course materials—syllabi, texts, assignments, and samples of student work—to faculty development events. Provide time during a one-day event or across a multiday institute for teaching teams to sit together to process what they have learned and to consider how they can apply curricular design principles and promising pedagogies to their individual communities.

Provide structures and opportunities for continuous planning. If your program has resources to allow for course reductions or release time the semester prior to or during a learning community assignment, develop a schedule for regular planning meetings. Discussions during the semester or quarter are especially important. Encourage teaching teams to communicate via e-mail or phone between meetings. Faculty teams need to see their community plan as dynamic—always changing and easily adaptable. Schön (1983) provides a useful analogy for thinking about planning: "When good jazz musicians improvise together, they also manifest a 'feel for' their material and they make on-the-spot adjustments to the sounds they hear. Listening to one another and to themselves, they feel where the music is going and adjust their playing accordingly" (p. 55).

Meet with individual teaching teams or host informal gatherings for program faculty to come together to talk about how things are going. Encourage improvisation in places where the community does not seem to be coming together or when particular assignments or class discussions may not be "playing" as well as anticipated.

Assessment and Reflection

Conversations about assessment should occur alongside decisions about curriculum and pedagogy. Teaching teams need to discuss intended outcomes for students and what they consider evidence of student learning. Direct evidence might include portfolios, rubrics for written work, scores on tests, and student reflections on what they have learned over the course of the class and community. Some examples of indirect evidence—indication that students are probably learning but what they are learning is less clear—could include transcript analysis, learning outcomes stated on syllabi, or graduate admissions rates (Suskie, 2003).

Assessment, particularly evidence of student learning, is a high priority for both faculty teaching in learning communities and campus administrators. At an annual summer workshop for faculty in Temple University's learning communities, Linda Suskie, the director of the Office of Assessment at Towson University, conducted a session on assessing student learning. Faculty explored innovative ways to assess student learning beyond tests and papers. They worked in small groups to develop learning outcomes, create assignments, design rubrics, and discuss prompts for student self-reflection. Sample prompts included

- Describe something major that you learned about yourself in this course.
- How do you feel about biology?
- What was your favorite aspect of this course? Why?
- If you were to start this course over, what would you do differently next time?
- What would you like to learn further about this subject or discipline?
- In what areas did you improve the most?
- What was the most useful or meaningful thing you learned in this course? [Suskie, 2003]

Faculty received a packet of handouts, and materials were posted on the learning communities website (http://www.temple.edu/lc/faculty_resources.html).

How will faculty know what is working in their learning community in terms of student learning, their teaching, and students' overall experience in the learning community? It is important to include information on classroom assessment in faculty development activities. *Classroom Assessment Techniques,* by Angelo and Cross (1993), is a valuable handbook of classroom assessment techniques (CATs). An effective way to model CATs while also collecting information on how faculty perceive a workshop or event is to use a classroom assessment technique at the beginning, middle, or end of a faculty development program. At a three-day institute for faculty teaching in the learning communities at Capital

Community College in Hartford, Connecticut, participants completed assessment exercises at different points in the institute. Prior to a discussion on curricular planning, faculty were asked to take a "Classroom Opinion Poll" to solicit their views on integrated curriculum, the goals of learning communities, and expectations for team teaching. At the conclusion of the first day of training, they completed another CAT, a "Self-Confidence Survey" designed to assess participants' confidence levels in terms of curricular planning.

One important goal of learning communities faculty development is to create communities of faculty who actively engage in learning about learning and are willing to share this knowledge with peers. Learning communities faculty development activities should mirror learning communities classrooms, with participants learning from each other, cross-disciplinary learning, and an open exchange of ideas. This is a challenge, since for many teachers, teaching as "doing" and teaching as "knowing" are very different.

Faculty should leave a faculty development event energized and refreshed. They should have a sense of renewal about their curriculum and pedagogy, and faculty development coordinators should have a sense of what faculty learned or gained from their participation. Time to reflect is an important part of this process. Use self-reflection writing prompts for faculty development participants or teachers who have concluded an experience of teaching in a learning community:

- How do you feel about yourself as a teacher?
- What was the most useful or meaningful thing you learned in this workshop?
- List three ways you think you have grown or developed as a teacher as a result of participating in learning communities.
- What problems did you encounter in this community? How did you solve them?
- If you were to teach in this community again, what would you do differently?
- Describe something major that you learned about your teaching or your students.
- What one assignment for this course or community was the most successful? Why? (adapted from Suskie, 2003)

Encourage faculty to keep journals of their thoughts as they move through faculty development events and experience teaching in a learning community. Conduct reflective interviews with faculty at the end of the term. What were their expectations for teaching in a learning community? What were the realities of their experience? Additional assessment strategies are presented in Chapter Six.

Types of Faculty Development Events

Consider the principles and the stages of development of learning communities when planning activities for faculty. Make practical decisions about where to use faculty development resources since resources are limited on most campuses. If you are just introducing learning communities, invest time and resources in educating faculty on the goals of learning communities and the value they can add to the undergraduate experience. If the goals are to sustain learning communities and energize faculty teaching in the program, find ways to support faculty in their planning and teaching.

Faculty development events can range from brown-bag lunch series to multiday, off-campus planning retreats. Two popular formats are the one-day workshop and multiday institutes. Many campuses concentrate resources for faculty development on the semester or summer prior to a learning communities teaching assignment. Single-day events coordinated on campus involving in-house speakers are less costly than the more expensive multiday retreats that occur off campus and feature outside consultants or experts. Decisions about the type and extent of faculty development will be greatly influenced by available resources. But even programs with limited funds must consider ways to support faculty teaching in learning communities. Work with an on-campus teaching and learning center, partner with other programs to share costs, or invite colleagues recognized on campus as good teachers or assessment experts to speak at a small learning communities gathering.

Presemester Workshops

A one-day workshop is an efficient, low-cost training format for established learning community programs with a returning corps of faculty or a mix of veteran and novice teachers. The agenda for a one-day workshop should include an introduction or overview of program goals and expectations, discussion of topics central to learning communities (collaborative learning, student development theory, group dynamics, classroom assessment), opportunities for small group work, time for teaching teams to talk about their courses and community, and time for assessment and reflection. Time is limited in this format, so consider preworkshop readings or assignments that can be sent to participants in advance. Suggested preworkshop readings include

- "Why Learning Communities? Why Now." (K. P. Cross) *About Campus* July–August 1998, *3*(3), 4–11.
- "Introducing Learning Communities to Your Campus" (N. S. Shapiro and J. H. Levine) *About Campus,* 1999, *4*(5).

- "Curricular Learning Communities." (J. H. Levine and N. S. Shapiro) In B. Jacoby, Ed., *Involving Commuter Students in Learning.* New Directions for Higher Education, no. 109. San Francisco: Jossey-Bass, 2000.
- "What Is Collaborative Learning?" (B. L. Smith and J. MacGregor) In A. S. Goodsell, M. R. Maher, and V. Tinto, Eds., *Collaborative Learning: A Sourcebook for Higher Education.* National Center on Postsecondary Teaching, Learning, and Assessment. University Park, PA, NCPTLA, Syracuse University, 1992.
- "Organizing for Learning: A New Imperative." (P. Ewell) In *AAHE Bulletin,* 1997, *50*(4), 3–6.
- "Taking Structure Seriously: The Learning Community Model." (B. L. Smith) *Liberal Education,* April 1993, *77*(2), 42–48.
- "Psychology in Context: Making Connections to Other Disciplines." (N. J. Finley) *Teaching of Psychology,* 1995, *22*(2), 105–108.
- "How Learning Communities Affect Students" (N. S. Shapiro and J. H. Levine) *Peer Review,* Summer/Fall 2001, *3/4*(4/1).

One-day workshops typically focus on the goals and expectations of the learning community program and on curriculum planning and pedagogy. Outside speakers can be brought in to address special topics such as collaborative learning, teaching with teams, uses of technology, or writing across the curriculum. Exhibit 5.2 is the agenda from a Temple University Learning Communities summer workshop.

Identify faculty on your own campus who are known for their teaching or have conducted research in areas of teaching, learning, or assessment. This is an excellent way to broaden participation of faculty in learning communities beyond those teaching in the program. For example, the Temple University learning community program invited the university writing director to discuss writing across the disciplines. Faculty from psychology conducted sessions on learning theory and motivation. Student affairs is another source for presenters. Consider inviting staff from the counseling center to talk about group dynamics or the needs of first-year college students. Individuals from residence life or activities can talk about learning opportunities outside the classroom.

Since time for curricular planning is limited in a one-day format, make sure there is a mechanism for follow-up. Teachers should exchange contact information and leave the workshop with agreed-upon times and dates to continue planning conversations. Temple University sponsors summer planning lunches as a follow-up to its one-day workshop. Teaching teams are invited to attend one of several planning sessions scheduled the weeks immediately following the summer workshop. On-campus space is reserved over lunchtime, snacks are

EXHIBIT 5.2. LEARNING COMMUNITIES FACULTY DEVELOPMENT WORKSHOP

8:30–9:30: **Breakfast for first-time learning communities faculty**
- Learning Communities Overview
- Words of Wisdom from LC Veterans

9:30–12:00 **Guest Speaker, Sandra Hurd, Syracuse University**
Enhancing Student Learning: Student Teams in Learning Communities

"Using Student Teams in Learning Communities"

Dr. Hurd is the Faculty Coordinator of the Learning Communities Program at Syracuse University and is a Professor of Law & Public Policy in the School of Management. A chapter from Dr. Hurd's book, *Using Student Teams in the Classroom,* is enclosed as a preworkshop reading.

12:00–12:30 **Lunch with your teaching team**

12:30–1:00 **Program Update**
- Fall 2001 Faculty Handbook
- Community Plans
- Summer and Fall Faculty Development Activities

1:00–2:00 **Lessons Learned from the Fall 2000 Learning Communities Experience Questionnaire**

2:00–3:00 **Free time for teaching team planning**

provided, and teaching teams can come together to discuss their courses and plan their community. Each teacher receives a small stipend for participating in a lunch discussion with his or her entire team. The overall goal is to motivate teaching teams to complete their community plan, a two-page worksheet describing the theme for the community and how the courses will be integrated.

Institutes and Retreats

Multiday institutes allow for more in-depth coverage of faculty development topics along with more time for curricular planning, team building, and reflection. These programs can be scheduled during the school year, at the end of a school year, or during the summer. Consult the faculty on your campus to determine when the maximum number of people can participate.

Multiday institutes typically begin with time for getting acquainted and team building. Icebreakers used with faculty can then be used with learning communities classes when the term begins. Set clear goals for the institute. Preinstitute readings can focus faculty participants on the major themes for the training. The institute curriculum should be a mix of presentations, workshops, small group activities, and team planning time. Each teaching team should leave the institute with a curricular plan that can be implemented for their learning community.

Using funds from a Title III grant, Capital Community College organizes two- to three-day institutes for faculty teaching in its learning communities program. Institute activities are divided into three areas: (1) curricular planning, (2) teaching practices, and (3) implementation issues. Teaching teams work together on a variety of activities designed to familiarize each other with their disciplines and courses. They are then given time to develop a community plan for their linked courses. Participants read case studies and discuss the issues and solutions in teams and as a full group. Case topics range from problems that arise when students are assigned group projects to what can happen when members of the faculty teaching team do not view their roles in similar ways.

Northampton Community College sponsored a two-day Learning Communities Summer Institute early in its planning to introduce faculty to the history, goals, models, uses, and curricular nature of learning communities. On day one, participants engaged in cross-disciplinary thinking. The goal for day two was to consider real possibilities for learning communities at the college. An external facilitator was invited to help participants design potential learning communities and to consider uses of learning communities at Northampton. All participants received a packet of readings and resources on learning communities. The summer institutes are an annual event at Northampton, with different emphases each spring. Other featured topics have included writing across the curriculum, critical thinking, assessment, and technology. The primary goal for each institute is the "introduction to new ideas/developments in postsecondary education for our teaching faculty" (J. Benner, personal communication, August 2001).

Institutes can also be open to non-learning communities faculty, a wonderful opportunity to extend the dialogue about teaching and learning across campus, as well as to increase awareness and faculty support for the learning communities. The University of Maryland's College Park Scholars program sponsored a two-day College Park Scholar's Institute to bring teachers together to talk about teaching and learning. The theme for the 2002 institute, "The Spirit of Teaching: More Than Words," examined the human aspects of teaching. The program included formal addresses, discussions with students, social activities with university leaders, and planned time for reflection and discussion.

Similar in format and content to multiday institutes, retreats typically take place at an off-campus location or retreat center. The time away provides a relaxed environment and therefore enhanced opportunities for team building and reflection. For more than fifteen years, the Washington Center for Improving the Quality of Undergraduate Education has sponsored curriculum planning retreats for teachers across Washington State who will be working together in learning communities. The retreats are organized so that teaching teams can work on their own, meet with experienced learning communities practitioners, and attend workshops. As described in retreat literature: "The grounding for all the workshops at the retreat is a commitment to create inclusive learning environments that enfranchise people from many different backgrounds" (J. MacGregor, personal communication, August 2001).

The February 2001 retreat for faculty at William Rainey Harper College was themed "Rendezvous with Teaching and Learning." The three-day event featured small group activities, guest speakers, and action planning. Exhibit 5.3 is the schedule-at-a-glance for the retreat.

LaGuardia Community College holds an annual spring retreat for its learning communities faculty. Goals for the event include (1) establishing connections across disciplines for the planning of future learning communities, (2) discussing administrative support issues, (3) sharing effective pedagogical strategies, and (4) introducing other timely topics. Participants do not receive a stipend, but the learning communities program pays all expenses, including meals and travel. The two-day retreat typically begins with dinner and welcome remarks, followed by an opening session. On day two, participants work in smaller groups around the topic introduced the prior evening. Immediately following the retreat, the program directors send participants notes from the brainstorming and action-planning sessions. This is an excellent way to keep faculty involved and focused on the program goals.

The College Park Scholars Program at the University of Maryland holds an annual midsemester retreat each January to address topics raised during the first half of the academic year. Teachers from across the living-learning programs come together to discuss experiences in their programs as well as process and management issues such as judicial affairs, academic honesty, diversity and multicultural sensitivity, technology, and student wellness.

EXHIBIT 5.3. WILLIAM RAINEY HARPER
COLLEGE FACULTY RETREAT

ITINERARY

Thursday	9:30	Arrive at Interlaken
	10:00–12:30	Session I—Creating a Learning Community Lichenstein Room (Downstairs)
	12:30–1:30	Lunch
	1:30–2:15	Session 2—Veterans Share Their Experiences
	2:15–2:45	Read Article
	2:45–3:30	Session 3—Lynn Secrest, What Does Our Future Hold Break and Vote
	3:30—5:00	Session 4—Small Group Breakout: Our Future
	5:00–7:00	Free Time
	7:00–8:00	Dinner
	8:00–10:00	Live Music in the Bar
Friday	8:00–9:00	Breakfast
	9:00–12:30	Session 5—Bernice McCarthy, Learning Styles
	10:30–11:00	Break
	12:30–1:30	Lunch
	1:30–5:00	Session 6—Bernice McCarthy, Learning Styles
	3:00–3:30	Break
	5:00–7:00	Free Time
	7:00–8:00	Dinner
	8:00–10:00	Storytelling Around Fireplace with Ben Yoder in Alpine Room
Saturday	8:00–9:00	Breakfast (Check Out—Leave Bags at Front Desk)
	9:00–10:30	Session 7—Hot Spot Small Groups Convene
	10:30–11:00	Break
	11:00–12:30	Session 8—Develop Action Plans
	GO HOME	

THANKS FOR ALL THE HARD WORK AND THE GREAT FUN!

In-semester Activities

When a campus opts to concentrate faculty development resources on pre-semester planning, opportunities for in-semester faculty development should also be planned. In-semester faculty development activities might include topical workshops, teaching circles, brown-bag lunch series, or informal gatherings to discuss how the semester or year is going. Learning communities leadership need not reinvent the wheel or duplicate existing programming when it comes to faculty development activities. If your campus has a teaching-learning center or instructional support center, encourage faculty to take part in scheduled events. Ask to cosponsor activities with other programs, schools, or colleges. Consider sending teams of faculty to regional or national conferences with tracks and sessions related to learning communities such as the first-year experience, faculty roles, pedagogy, assessment, or writing.

LaGuardia Community College follows its spring retreat with its opening sessions workshops in the fall. The workshops provide an opportunity for follow-up discussions from the spring retreat but also an opportunity to involve more faculty in learning communities. Opening sessions workshops participants are typically individuals interested in getting involved in learning communities. Presenters are people either currently active in learning communities or those about to teach in a cluster. In addition to these opening sessions workshops, throughout the year the program sponsors poster sessions in which those teaching in learning communities can share what they are doing with each other and discuss common issues or concerns. Individuals interested in proposing a cluster are encouraged to attend these sessions as well (P. VanSlyck, personal communication, December 2001).

Opening learning communities events to faculty not teaching in learning communities is an effective strategy for connecting the program to the campus and faculty culture. It is an ideal setting for learning communities teachers to gather with their faculty colleagues to explore common goals for their teaching and students. Faculty who might be skeptical of learning communities, or the types of teaching commonly practiced in communities, may come to realize that learning communities can be a structure to help them achieve their goals. This is helpful for recruiting new teachers to the program and increasing campuswide support for learning communities (B. Midden, personal communication, August 2003).

The National Learning Communities Project sponsors annual summer institutes at the Evergreen State College. The four-day learning community institute, held in June, is an ideal opportunity for campus teams to plan a learning community initiative or focus on strengthening or expanding an existing program. Approximately twenty teams are selected to participate through an application process. The institute features workshops, team planning time, and consultations with national learning communities leaders [http://learningcommons. evergreen.edu/institute.asp].

Additional Resources for Faculty

In planning faculty development activities, consider the resources that will be made available to teachers. Many programs develop faculty handbooks, websites, resource rooms, or listservs/discussion boards to encourage ongoing faculty development and communication.

Faculty Handbooks

A faculty handbook is a useful guide to good practice in learning communities. Handbook content can reinforce program expectations and faculty roles. The handbook can include information on curricular planning, teaching tips, and assessment strategies. Include sample planning documents and syllabi from past learning community teaching teams. Invite former learning communities faculty to author essays on their experiences teaching in communities. Faculty also find it useful to have information on campus resources, such as where to refer students with financial aid problems or questions about degree requirements.

Faculty members teaching in Temple University's learning communities are given a copy of the faculty handbook at the annual summer workshop. The handbook is also available online (www.temple.edu/lc). The handbook includes an essay describing definitions and models of learning communities, along with a summary of focus group research (reflective interviews) on how faculty perceive the rewards and challenges of teaching in a learning community.

Websites

A website is a valuable, virtual handbook. Through a website, program faculty can access information about the program goals, services, and resources. Many learning communities websites are designed for internal and external audiences and for participating students as well as faculty.

The University of South Florida website (http://w3.usf.edu/~lc/sitemap. html) includes announcements and a link to a faculty discussion list. There is also an administration and staff directory with e-mail links. Content is divided into ten areas:

- Faculty
- Advising
- USF Learning Communities
- Strategic Instructional Methods
- Writing Across the Curriculum
- Information Literacy and Instructional Technologies
- Assessment
- Learning Community Alumni
- Research, Publications, and Conferences (Dissemination)
- Grants

Under Faculty, teachers can find information on planning strategies for team teaching, faculty roles, integrated curriculum, and development of assignments that stimulate thinking. The Strategic Instructional Methods section covers topics such as historical literacy, developing cognitive skills, and instructional support systems on campus.

The Integrated Learning Garden (http://www.mcli.dist.maricopa.edu/ilc/ index.html), the learning communities website for the Maricopa Community Colleges in Arizona, is a useful site for learning communities teachers at Maricopa and for the national learning communities audience. The site contains information on models and components of learning communities. There is also a link to "Learning Communities: Getting Started," Geri Rasmussen and Elizabeth Skinner's (2001) monograph on planning a learning community. The site also features quotes from students and links to the various learning community programs at the Maricopa system campuses.

Discussion Lists

Discussion lists or listservs are an effective way to promote communication among learning communities teachers and to share information with faculty. Develop a program listserv to encourage dialogue on topics of interest to faculty teaching in your program. This list can also be used to announce upcoming campus events and faculty development activities, reminders about registration deadlines for students, and information on academic support resources for students. Set up individual program or community lists for communication among individual teaching teams. Two national listservs that discuss learning communities are the Learning Communities Leaders List (learncom@ listserv.temple.edu) and the Residential Learning Communities and Living-Learning Programs List (reslearncomllp@listproc.bgsu.edu).

Resource Rooms

If space allows, build a resource area for program faculty. Create a welcoming space that faculty will want to visit and where they can talk with other faculty and read journals and books related to their work in learning communities. Exhibit 5.4 is a list for learning communities teachers. Readings should cover a range of topics related to teaching and learning:

- Effective teaching practices
- Assessing student learning
- Diversity
- Fostering student involvement and engagement
- Teaching as a profession
- Civic engagement
- Student development
- Faculty development

Making resources available to faculty is an efficient way to extend faculty development beyond traditional gatherings such as institutes and workshops. When assembling resources for faculty, invite current and former teachers in the program to suggest materials that they considered helpful. Visit websites of other learning communities programs to see what other campuses make available to learning communities teachers.

Evaluation of Faculty Development Programs

It is important to assess faculty development programs for purposes of short- and long-term program improvement. End-of-session evaluations or interviews can be used to gather feedback from faculty on the types of activities they find appealing and useful. Faculty can also describe how they are applying what they have learned to their teaching and classroom management.

EXHIBIT 5.4. WHAT LEARNING COMMUNITIES FACULTY ARE READING

- Brookfield and Preskill (1999), *Discussion as a Way of Teaching*
- Brookfield (2000), *The Skillful Teacher*
- Campbell and Smith, eds. (1997), *New Paradigms for College Teaching*
- Cross and Steadman (1997), *Classroom Research*
- Finkel (2000), *Teaching with Your Mouth Shut*
- Gabelnick, MacGregor, Matthews, and Smith (1990), *Learning Communities: Creating Connections Among Students, Faculty and Disciplines*
- Guarasci and Cornwell (1997), *Democratic Education in an Age of Difference: Redefining Citizenship in Higher Education*
- Huba and Freed (1999), *Learner-Centered Assessment on College Campuses: Shifting the Focus from Teaching to Learning*
- Light (2001), *Making the Most of College: Students Speak Their Minds*
- McKeachie (2002, 11th ed.), *McKeachie's Teaching Tips: Strategies, Research and Theory for College and University Teachers*
- Millis and Cottell (1998), *Cooperative Learning for Higher Education Faculty*
- Palmer (1998), *The Courage to Teach*
- Parks Daloz, Keen, Keen, and Daloz Parks (1997), *Common Fire: Leading Lives of Commitment in a Complex World*
- Schoem and Hurtado (2001), *Intergroup Dialogue: Deliberative Democracy in School, Community and Workplace*
- Schon (1983), *The Reflective Practitioner: How Professionals Think in Action*
- Shapiro and Levine (1999), *Creating Learning Communities: A Practical Guide to Winning Support, Organizing for Change, and Implementing Programs*
- Silverman and Casazza (1999), *Learning and Development: Making Connections to Enhance Teaching*
- Smith and McCann (2001), *Reinventing Ourselves: Interdisciplinary Education, Collaborative Learning, and Experimentation in Higher Education*
- Stein and Hurd (2000), *Using Student Teams in the Classroom*
- Wiggins and McTighe (1998), *Understanding by Design*
- Wlodkowski and Ginsberg (1995), *Diversity and Motivation: Culturally Responsive Teaching*

End-of-workshop, institute, or retreat evaluations can assist program leadership in improving future events. How were speakers received? What segments of the program did faculty find most valuable? Assessment tools can range from homegrown instruments with closed- or open-ended items to simple classroom assessment techniques that teachers can then use in their own classrooms. Give participants an index card and ask them to respond briefly to two questions: (1) What did you learn today that you can use in your learning community? (2) What questions remain unanswered? A listserv is an effective way to follow up on remaining questions or concerns.

Survey program faculty to identify topics of interest for future events. In-semester activities such as brown-bag lunches, lecture series, or short workshops can be organized around topics that faculty rate as being timely and relevant to their professional development. Consider focus groups or interviews to gather information on changes in teaching practices. What changes have faculty members made to their teaching as a result of participating in learning communities? Are they assessing student learning in new or different ways? What changes have they made to their non-learning communities courses as a result of faculty development or the learning communities experience? Assessment of faculty development should be included in the evaluation of the overall learning community program.

Conclusion

Faculty development for learning communities takes place at the personal, professional, and program levels. In addition to emphasizing individual growth and teaching skills, faculty and instructional development for learning communities addresses the expectations and goals for learning communities, community building, pedagogy that promotes learning in and from community, integrated curriculum design, and collaborative learning. It is an ongoing process that begins with presemester planning, extends through the semester, and allows time for assessment and reflection at the conclusion of the experience. Most important, it is teacher-centered: teachers are encouraged to learn from each other. Good faculty development recognizes that teachers come to programs with rich experiences and knowledge drawn from their students, peers, and own teaching or research. Faculty development in learning communities leads to the creation of faculty communities—supportive environments in which teachers share knowledge, learn new techniques, practice innovative pedagogy, and assess their progress with their peers.

CHAPTER SIX

DEVELOPING PURPOSEFUL AND
FOCUSED ASSESSMENT

Assessment of learning communities occurs at various levels: in individual programs or communities, across communities, and of the larger learning community program. It is assessment of the intended outcomes for students, faculty, and the institution. This chapter discusses various approaches or foci for evaluating learning communities at all of the levels.

Many of the examples of learning communities evaluation in this chapter try to answer questions of impact, the "what" of a program: What is the impact on students? What do teachers experience? What are the differences across communities or types of communities? This chapter includes examples of evaluation and assessment carried out by stakeholders invested in learning communities—program leadership, those teaching in the program, or colleagues on campus with research interests related to learning communities. Perhaps most important, the illustrations describe how lessons learned led to substantive changes and improvements. Data collection methods differ across the examples, although several campuses relied on survey or qualitative approaches in "an effort to understand situations in their uniqueness as part of particular context and the interactions there" (Merriam and others, 2002, p. 5).

Defining the Purpose

Ongoing evaluation is central to the implementation and maintenance of learning community programs. Good learning communities assessment occurs in stages; it progresses from formative assessment in the early years to more systematic, summative evaluations. A common tendency is to postpone evaluation until program leaders feel they are completely established, successful, and worthy. Evaluative activities, however, should begin before the first learning community is ever scheduled, before faculty start planning or students enroll. Evaluation begins with needs assessment and progresses to formative evaluation, evaluation for purposes of collecting data that are used primarily for purposes of program improvement. Assessment is not a stand-alone phase of learning communities planning but rather a set of activities conducted concurrently with decisions about implementing, developing, and sustaining a program.

Jacobs (1988), whose work with the evaluation of family and community programs was part of the emergence of the professionalization of program evaluation, outlined five basic assumptions about the purpose and value of program evaluation:

- Evaluation should be viewed as the systematic collection and analysis of program-related data.
- Evaluation is a necessary component to every program, regardless of its size, age, and orientation.
- There are numerous legitimate purposes for evaluation.
- There are many legitimate audiences for an evaluation.
- Evaluation activities should not detract from service delivery [p. 49].

Learning communities practitioners struggling with the questions of what or when to assess need to remember that although assessment is a natural part of program development and maintenance, there is no one-size-fits-all protocol or approach. These basic assumptions about assessment are intended to guide assessment planning. From here assessment decisions are made based on the purposes for learning communities, the stage of program development, as well as the resources—human and fiscal—available for assessment.

Jacobs (1988) offers a useful, five-tiered approach to program evaluation that "organizes evaluation activities at five levels, each requiring greater efforts at data collection and tabulation, increased precision in program definition, and a greater commitment to the evaluation process" (p. 50). This model can be adapted for planning the evaluation of learning communities. Level One, the preimplementation tier, focuses on the need for learning communities and sets the stage for future assessment. Level Two, the accountability tier, involves program monitoring, including specific information about who uses the program. Level Three is the program clarification tier. This level relies on information collected during tiers one and two, along with feedback from faculty and students, to monitor and improve learning communities. Level Four focuses on progress toward objectives. The focus here is primarily on program effectiveness, whereas Level Five–the program impact tier– relies on more rigorous, summative evaluation to identify and measure the short- and long-term impact of learning communities. Outcomes might include expectations for student learning, faculty teaching, institutional change, or a combination of these or other locally defined outcomes. Table 6.1 outlines this approach.

Jacobs (1988) advises that although the tiers are sequential, programs can and should engage in multiple levels of evaluation concurrently and revisit an earlier level as needed. For example, Learning Communities at Temple University celebrated its tenth year in 2002–2003. The program was initiated in 1993 to create community at a large university and to improve teaching and learning in the first year. About five years into the program, conversations with faculty and students began to reveal a shift in the goals and purposes of the program, as well as a lack of clarity and agreement on what learning communities were supposed to do. Early assessment revealed that participation in learning communities successfully augmented student retention and satisfaction. The assessment priorities therefore could shift to focus more on teaching and learning. For the program, and across the individual communities, there was a need to create opportunities for richer, more meaningful learning and to provide greater interaction between students and teachers around academic matters. After reviewing data from focus group interviews with faculty and two years of student survey data, the program goals were revised. Faculty development activities and program literature were organized around three new goals: (1) integration of knowledge, (2) transition to college-level learning, and (3) connections between and among students and teachers.

Determining a Focus

According to Patton (1997)–an interdisciplinary evaluation generalist whose books on qualitative, utilization-focused, and practical evaluation have influenced the evaluation movement in education–program evaluation is "the systematic collection of information about the activities, characteristics, and outcomes of programs to make judgments about the program, improve program effectiveness, and/or inform decisions about future programming" (p. 23). He argues that program evaluation goes beyond determining whether or not a program has met its stated goals; it also examines implementation, processes, unanticipated outcomes and consequences, and long-term effect. Programs can learn a great deal by asking, What else is happening here?

TABLE 6.1. A TIERED APPROACH TO EVALUATING LEARNING COMMUNITIES

Level	Tier	Purpose	Audiences	Tasks
1	Preimplementation	1. Document needed for learning communities within the institution 2. Demonstrate the fit between institution needs and learning communities goals 3. Collect "data groundwork" (baseline information)	1. Potential approvers—those who need to approve and/or fund learning communities 2. Other stakeholders: faculty, students, staff	1. Outline basic characteristics of learning communities 2. Conduct a basic campus needs assessment to support the implementation of learning communities 3. Revise the proposed program according to the campus needs assessment
2	Accountability	1. Document program's use, position, and penetration within the targeted population 2. Justify current expenditures and/or an increase in funding 3. Build a constituency	1. Approvers 2. Supporters 3. Community leaders	1. Describe the program 2. Provide accurate cost information
3	Program clarification	1.Provide information to program leadership and participants to improve learning communities	1. Program leadership 2. Faculty, students, staff	1. Clarify who experiences what and how 2. Clarify and restate program's missions, goals, objectives, and strategies

Level	Tier	Purpose	Audiences	Tasks
4	Progress toward objectives	1. Provide information for program improvement 2. Document program effectiveness	1. Program leadership 2. Faculty, students, staff 3. Approvers, funders 4. Other programs	1. Examine outcomes objectives 2. Derive indicators of success for the objectives 3. Decide on data analysis methods 4. Assess effectiveness among different participants
5	Program impact	1. Produce evidence of effectiveness 2. Contribute to knowledge development in the field of learning communities 3. Suggest models or strategies worth replicating	1. Academic and research communities 2. Learning communities practitioners 3. General higher education community	1. Outline specific impact objectives 2. Identify measures to assess enduring changes among participants

Good evaluation must be useful to some audience, be feasible and realistic in scope, be conducted ethically and fairly, and be accurate (Patton, 1997). It can begin with a simple fill-in-the-blank exercise: "I would really like to know _____ about the Learning Communities Program or about our learning community" (p. 30). In any evaluation, there are many potential audiences or uses for results.

"Utilization-focused evaluation requires moving from the general and abstract, that is possible audiences and potential uses, to the real and specific: actual primary intended users and their explicit commitments to concrete, specific uses" (p. 21). This type of evaluation is personal and situational. A team of learning communities faculty may choose to investigate how students apply interdisciplinary knowledge to an end-of-semester project on literacy in urban school children. The level of understanding emerging from student work would be used to modify the curricular design for a subsequent semester or quarter. In addition to the teaching team, other audiences for this evaluation might include students

(What is the level of understanding teachers expect students to achieve in the community? For this assignment?) and other faculty teaching in learning communities (What are the characteristics of a successful interdisciplinary assignment?).

Patton (1997) outlines alternative types and focuses of evaluations. Some approaches or focuses applicable to learning communities include

- *Collaborative approach.* Evaluators and intended audiences work together on the evaluation.
- *Context focus.* What is the environment within which the program operates politically, socially, economically, culturally? How does this context affect program effectiveness?
- *Critical issues focus.* Critical issues and concerns of primary intended users focus the evaluation (diversity, citizenship, achievement in math).
- *Descriptive focus.* What happens in the program?
- *Effectiveness focus.* To what extent is the learning communities program meeting its goals?
- *Needs assessment.* What do students or teachers need, and how can those needs be met?
- *Outcomes evaluation.* To what extent are desired student, teacher, or institutional outcomes being realized? What are the effects of learning communities on participants?
- *Process focus.* What do participants experience in the program? What are the strengths and weaknesses of the daily or regular happenings?
- *Question focus.* What do primary intended users want to know that would make a difference to what they do (emphasis on answers instead of judgments)?

Determining which approach to use depends on several factors. First, assessment knowledge and resources: What are your assessment skills? Who is available to assist with assessment and evaluation? What are the costs? What is the timeline? An end-of-semester survey requires less time than a longitudinal study, which by definition takes years to complete. Audience is another important consideration. Will the information be used internally for program-level decisions or are data being requested by an external audience for accountability purposes? The needs of a program are another variable to consider. A new program may require basic information on who enrolls in learning communities. A question-focused approach would meet this purpose. A more established program looking to provide more support for teachers in communities might consider an effectiveness-focused evaluation to see whether current faculty development efforts are meeting teachers' needs.

Collaborative Approach

By definition, learning communities engage teachers and students as partners in the teaching and learning process. It is logical and natural, therefore, to extend the collaboration to assessment. Faculty members will be more vested in program improvement if they are involved in the planning, implementation, and review of evaluative activities.

Temple University formed an assessment work group of teachers in learning communities, program leadership, and the university's director of Measurement and Research to examine the student experience in learning communities. The group met several times to discuss the goals of learning communities and to review existing instruments for measuring student learning and classroom experiences. The collaboration proved useful in many ways, but an unintended aspect of the project yielded the most helpful information. In earlier discussions on what the group wanted to assess, it quickly become apparent that there was a need for clarification on what learning communities were supposed to do. Were the primary goals intellectual or social in nature, or both? Was the learning community classroom experience supposed to be different from a non-learning community classroom, and if so, in what ways?

Input from learning communities teachers shaped the development of a questionnaire designed to examine the types of learning and social activities in which learning communities students engaged, as well as the extent to which students described the helpfulness of these activities to their learning. An open-ended item was included to learn how students described the curricular theme for their communities and how they perceived the extent of the curricular integration between the linked courses. Results (Jones, Morris, Levine, and Foley, 2002) showed that whereas students did recognize curricular connections and academic benefits, they perceived the benefits of enrolling in a community to be primarily social—forming friendships, meeting new people, and socializing with peers.

The collaborative nature of this project extended beyond assessment and into faculty development. Guided by the results from the first two administrations of the questionnaire, a faculty development work group redesigned the goals of the learning communities and created new materials to disseminate and describe these goals to students and faculty in learning communities. The new goals—integration of knowledge, transition to college-level learning, and formation of connections between and among students and teachers—now focus more specifically on the academic objectives that can be achieved through partnerships of students and teachers.

Context Focus

A context-focused evaluation examines the environment in which the program exists. In early assessment of its learning communities, Skagit Valley College uncovered a problem regarding the learning communities requirement for students in professional and technical programs. Surveys were conducted with students on Skagit's Whidbey Island and Mount Vernon campuses (Dunlap and Stanwood, 1996). Twelve questions addressed completion of the learning communities requirement, scheduling, and barriers. "Over half of the students found it moderately or seriously difficult to schedule [a learning community]. Interestingly, though, only 16.5 percent cited scheduling as their main concern. Most found that the [communities] offered did not pertain directly to their program or employability" (L. Dunlap, personal communication, September 2002).

This discovery led to ongoing investigations as to whether the learning communities requirement was an obstacle to graduation for some students. It was clear that we had not laid the groundwork for learning communities in these programs as thoughtfully and thoroughly as we had in transfer programs. Several studies noted that the narrow definition of learning communities left many faculty feeling excluded from the opportunity to participate. It became evident as well that the college had no mechanism for assuring success of collaborative courses in some delivery methods, for example, in evening and distance classes, and that students did not fully understand the degree requirements and the rationale for collaborative courses (Stanwood and Dunlap, 2003).

To address these and other issues related not only to learning communities but also to the college's general education program, Skagit made revisions to its degree and modified its goals for learning communities. Technical students were no longer required to take learning communities, and Skagit adjusted its definition of learning communities to allow for more options. Subsequent options for learning communities allow combinations of courses from departments in the same discipline or combinations of developmental, technical, or skill courses. Skagit realized that it needed to examine and consider the context of its learning communities in order to maximize the potential for developing rich and stimulating environments for faculty, sharing pedagogy, creating academic and social relationships among students, strengthening interpersonal skills, and allowing students to explore diverse points of view (Stanwood and Dunlap, 2003).

Critical Issues Focus

A critical issues–focused evaluation is closely tied to the specific objectives for implementing learning communities. (Chapter Two discusses the importance of setting clear goals and objectives.) Focused objectives might include diversity, citizenship education, achievement in science or math, or applications of technology.

Students in George Mason's New Century College experience a curriculum that integrates teaching and learning around nine competencies: communication, valuing, effective citizenship, critical thinking, group interaction, aesthetic response, problem solving, global perspective, and information technology. The information technology competency is defined as: "Understand and use current information technology applications based on computers and networks. Able to master basic skills to acquire, organize, and apply information using databases, spreadsheets, word and information processing, presentation graphics; evaluate the effectiveness and reliability of various information sources for their appropriate use. Critical awareness of public policy issues relating to information technology" (Montecino, Smith, and Young, 2000, p. 1).

Technology learning experiences for first-year students in New Century College include electronic communication, library catalog and database searching, web-page creation, presentation design, and data manipulation. Students' use of information technology was assessed via day-to-day assignments and an information technology survey. At the beginning and end of the year, students completed a survey designed to measure their experience with information technology (IT) and to calculate an IT literacy quotient. From the pre- to post-administration of the survey, students reported a considerable change in their experience with information technology, with the greatest increases in the use of file transfer protocol, html, statistical software, listservs, and presentation software (Montecino, Smith, and Young, 2000).

Data collected through this evaluative effort helped New Century College identify future directions not only for information technology but also for other aspects of the curriculum: "We still need to do a better job of integrating IT concepts and assessment at all levels of our curriculum. . . . As with all [New Century College] competencies, IT is best absorbed when placed in context of other course or curricular themes" (Montecino, Smith, and Young, 2000, p. 7). The study also reinforced the need to improve knowledge and use of information technology among the faculty. "Peer teaching and learning will help [New Century College] faculty become more comfortable assessing the technological knowledge and ability of our students" (p. 7).

Descriptive Focus

Descriptive evaluation focuses on the "what" and not the "why" or cause-and-effect aspects of a program (Patton, 1997). UCLA's College of Letters and Science assessment of its interdisciplinary team-taught general education clusters focused on the experiences of students, faculty, and graduate student instructors (TAs or teaching assistants) in the courses. They used surveys and interviews to describe each group of participants' learning communities experiences in seven areas: (1) incentives, (2) workload, (3) intellectual development, (4) community, (5) productivity, progress, and achievement, (6) enthusiasm and intellectual excitement, and (7) recognition and external rewards (p. 5). To assess the experiences of TAs, they conducted focus groups to gather information on the TAs' experiences and perceptions of issues related to the clusters. Teaching assistants lead two discussion sections or labs in the fall and winter clusters. Program leadership provides orientation workshops to train and prepare the TAs for their teaching experience.

The study revealed that the TAs choose to participate in clusters for the opportunity to teach a seminar in the spring quarter. Other incentives they described included working with distinguished faculty, working with the same students over an entire academic year, teaching in an interdisciplinary course, and securing yearlong funding (p. 28). In terms of workload, the TAs felt that teaching in a cluster took more time than other TA positions, in that out of class they spent more time on preparation and meetings and in class on synthesizing interdisciplinary material. The TAs described their students' intellectual development as well as their own. TAs gained

- Greater insights into curriculum development
- A keener appreciation of the challenges of teaching interdisciplinary courses
- A store of useful pedagogical tools
- Better ability to teach writing [College of Letters and Science, UCLA, 2001, p. 30]

How the TAs described "community" varied across the clusters. When the TAs were involved in planning for the clusters, they expressed a greater sense of community. Overall, the TAs were generally enthusiastic about their cluster experiences.

Effectiveness Focus

Evaluation with an effectiveness focus looks at how the program is doing in terms of meeting its goals and objectives. Students at Wagner College enroll in three learning communities across their undergraduate experiences. The first-year program includes a learning community, along with experiential learning, writing intensive tutors, academic advising, co-curricular activities, and residential living. The Wagner plan seeks to connect students to each other, their teachers, and the campus community. A faculty member from the freshman fall learning community serves as the student's academic adviser for the first year. Here are the goals of the Wagner Plan for the Practical Liberal Arts as described on the Wagner website (http://www.wagner.edu/prosstud/ugradstud/academics.html):

> Whether you are interested in a career as a scientist, business executive, psychologist or music critic, to be fully educated, it is important to have a strong liberal arts education as the underlying foundation for all academic study.
>
> A liberal arts education opens students' minds to the possibilities of thought and action. It provides students with the analytical skills necessary for effective problem solving. It allows students to understand the past while visualizing a future beyond the limits of human possibilities.
>
> In its best form, a liberal arts education is anchored in the real world. Our curriculum, The Wagner Plan for the Practical Liberal Arts, allows students to reach their academic, personal and professional potential and goals by incorporating real world experiences with a strong liberal arts curriculum. The Wagner Plan fosters dialog between disciplines by linking courses directly through Learning Communities so that real connections can be made across the curriculum and among students.
>
> True learning emerges from the study and communication of ideas, and seeing these ideas in practice; these are the goals of The Wagner Plan.

Wagner conducted learning community surveys from 1998 to 2002 to assess the student experience in learning communities. Students first complete a learning communities survey at the end of their fall semester first-year learning community experience. Annually, survey results have improved and stabilized. Results show that students maintain contact with their adviser and don't feel lost or disconnected from the campus (J. Barchitta, personal communication, September 2002). From 1999 to 2001, students increasingly responded that they felt their courses shared a common theme.

> If we focus on the data from 1999–2001, we find that students on average agree or strongly agree with items relating to positive academic experiences. They agreed that they have been given ample opportunity to actively participate in Learning Communities. They felt more connected to the students in their Learning Communities than to students in other courses. They had been challenged to improve their communication skills in the Learning Communities through reading, writing, and speaking. They found the courses in the Learning Communities to be well connected through a common theme. The

Learning Communities gave them opportunities to communicate more easily with faculty as professors and advisors [J. Barchitta, personal communication, September 2002].

An effectiveness focus can also reveal what is not working. Wagner's early student surveys on the experiential component of the first-year program revealed that students were not happy with their site locations and the logistics of getting from campus to their experiential learning site. As a result, a grant was written to obtain a van to help with transportation. After 1998, the number of students who agreed or strongly agreed that experiential learning was beneficial increased.

In their sophomore year, Wagner students typically enroll in their second learning community, the Intermediate Learning Community. Surveys show that the effectiveness of these communities vary by semester. Students who participate in spring intermediate communities feel more connected and see greater connections between the courses than students who take an intermediate community in a fall semester. Program leadership attributes this to the extent to which teachers participate in learning communities and how they are trained. Faculty members teaching in the spring Intermediate Learning Communities are often the same teachers participating in the fall First-Year Learning Communities. In the early years of implementing the Wagner Plan, faculty training activities primarily concentrated on the first-year component. When faculty involved in First-Year Learning Communities teach the Intermediate Learning Communities, the community experience is more effective (J. Barchitta, personal communication, September 2002). From this evaluation, Wagner identified a need to provide more faculty development for those teaching in Intermediate Learning Communities who have not had the training and experience of teaching in the first-year program.

Needs Assessment

Small group instructional diagnoses with students and reflective interviews with faculty are effective ways to gather information on what students and teachers need and how these needs can be met at the individual, community, and program levels. Needs assessment lays the foundation for a more comprehensive effectiveness evaluation by first examining basic implementation issues and identifying areas for improvement (Patton, 1997).

The Small Group Instructional Diagnosis is a structured interview process conducted midway through the course to solicit information from students on what helps them learn and how the class can be improved (White, 1995) (http://www.evergreen.edu/washcenter/resources/acl/c4.html). The brief, twenty-five-minute interview is conducted by a trained facilitator. Students are divided into small groups and discuss two questions: (1) What helps you learn in this course? (2) What improvements would you like, and how would you suggest they be made? Each group then reports two or three main ideas for each question to the facilitator and entire class. This collaborative, active approach to gathering information is particularly suited to learning communities.

Reflective interviews are another tool for needs assessment. Reflective or postprogram interviews with faculty provide an opportunity for teachers to reflect on the challenges and successes of teaching in a learning community. They also offer an opportunity for teachers to share lessons they learned that may help with subsequent planning or that can be useful to other faculty teaching in learning communities (Bystrom, 1995).

The Learning Communities Program at Temple University conducted reflective interviews with small groups of learning communities faculty at the end of the fall 2001 semester to assess the current needs of those teaching in the program. Modeled after the reflective interviews conducted at the Evergreen State College in Olympia, Washington, and by other learning community programs, the sessions were designed to give faculty an opportunity to debrief with program leadership on their experiences teaching in a linked-course learning community. Teachers were invited to share their expectations, observations, discoveries, and experiences. Faculty were asked:

1. What were your original expectations for teaching in this learning community program? Given those expectations, in what ways did the experience meet or not meet them?
2. What else stands out in terms of observations and discoveries? What did you notice about your students, colleagues' teaching, and your own teaching?
3. What issues need attention in the future: What might future learning community teaching teams consider? What might the program or institution consider and address?
4. As a result of teaching in this program, what will you take forward in your work?

These interviews revealed the clear need for better articulation of the expectations for "curricular coordination." Teachers expressed a need to better understand the expectations for curricular planning in linked-course learning communities, particularly, "What are teachers asked to do?" (Levine Laufgraben, 2003). Time for planning and assistance in coordinating planning was also discussed. Faculty commented that planning is problematic unless all teachers are involved or equally invested. Program leadership needs to ensure that teaching assignments are made in a timely and efficient manner.

As a result of feedback provided during the reflective interviews, several program improvements were instituted. Program goals were revisited and new goals widely disseminated. The website was enhanced to include a resources section for teachers, and new structures for faculty development and curricular planning were created. The community plan—a presemester worksheet outlining the curricular, pedagogical, and assessment components of a learning community—was updated to include a midsemester report version. (See Chapter Three for an example of the Temple Midsemester Report.) Teachers now meet regularly in the middle of the semester to discuss student progress and review curricular goals.

Outcomes Evaluation

Planning for an outcomes-focused evaluation begins long before any data are actually collected. It is predicated on clearly defined, agreed-upon, and articulated outcomes for learning communities. At Iowa State University, assessment was organized around a profile of learning outcomes. Desired learning communities outcomes for students included

- Higher academic achievement
- Greater use of university resources
- Increased interactions with faculty and staff
- More readily achieved learner outcomes
- Greater rate of persistence
- Greater satisfaction with academic experience [Alexander and others, 1999]

The Iowa State University Undergraduate Education Survey (http://www. iastate.edu/~learncommunity/assessment.html) was administered to measure students' satisfaction with their academic experiences, understanding of cultural differences, awareness of resources, interactions with students, faculty, and staff, and understanding of career options. Student perceptions were addressed in the areas of knowledge and abilities, allocation of time, values regarding the college experience, and satisfaction with various aspects of the learning environment.

Pre- and posttest versions of the survey were administered to learning communities and non-learning communities first-time freshmen. The survey revealed that at the onset of the school year, learning communities and non-learning communities students were looking forward to like experiences while worried about the same concerns (Huba, Epperson, and McFadden, 2000). They also expected to be spending about the same time in classes, studying, and participating in various campus activities. The non-learning communities students expected to work more hours than the learning community students, and the learning community students anticipated spending more time studying with peers, talking with an adviser, and taking part in service or volunteer activities.

There were greater differences between the two groups at the end of the semester. In terms of use of time, the learning community students spent significantly more time than their non-learning communities peers studying in groups, talking with instructors outside of class, talking with advisers, participating in leadership activities, and participating in service or volunteer work. The learning communities students also reported greater involvement in activities that promote learning and retention: earning higher grades, having professors with high expectations, receiving prompt feedback about their academic progress, having experiences that helped them reach their goals, and understanding the nature of their major (p. 6).

On other dimensions of the academic experience, learning communities students also reported greater satisfaction, including opportunities to interact with faculty, encouragement and advice from faculty, opportunities to collaborate with other students on class projects, and opportunities to apply learning to real-world problems and to practice skills. Students also reported greater satisfaction with the quality of instruction and the overall quality of their classmates (p. 7). Students reported that participating in a learning community did not lead to more opportunities to interact with students from different cultural backgrounds or to spend more time in recreational or social activities. Forming new friendships did, however, lead to more time studying with peers.

Process Focus

A process-directed evaluation looks at what's happening within a program and how aspects of a program fit together. "Process evaluation is developmental, descriptive, continuous, flexible, and inductive" (Patton, 1997, p. 206). Writing across the curriculum is an important component of the University of South Florida's learning communities program. During focus groups, students in the team-taught interdisciplinary learning communities expressed frustration that the faculty in their programs were grading papers differently. Process evaluation looks at what participants experience in terms of the "strengths and weaknesses of daily operations," such as grading. As a result of this feedback, USF sought to collect information on what teachers and students were experiencing in terms of writing instruction and writing achievement. "Because writing was taught within the context of different disciplines and faculty outside the English department were involved with writing instruction, LC students were not experiencing traditional freshman composition" (Flateby, 2003).

As part of the assessment of the University of South Florida Learning Community Program, Flateby and Metzger of USF developed the Cognitive Level and Quality of Writing Assessment (CLAQWA). The CLAQWA is a tool to help guide the teacher in selecting the thinking skills expected in writing assignments and in assessing the skills produced in students' writing (Flateby and Metzger, 2001). It was designed specifically for use by teachers whose primary discipline is not English or writing. The instrument helps students better understand what is expected of their writing. "After receiving feedback on the CLAQWA regarding specific writing skills, students recognize their strengths and weaknesses and are better prepared to revise their papers. Growth is readily apparent when instructors use the CLAQWA" (p. 5).

In the particular class or community, the teacher can use the CLAQWA to identify skill objectives. They can decide to examine skills in one or more categories (organization and development, language, grammar and mechanics, adequacy of assignments). Once the teacher identifies skills, the information is discussed with the students. The papers are marked according to the skill scale of the CLAQWA. Students comment that this "demystifies" grading (T. Flateby, personal communication, August 2002). At the program level, USF is now using the CLAQWA as part of larger assessment efforts to examine the cognitive level, writing skills, and intellectual development of learning communities participants. Early results show that learning communities students show greater progress in the development aspect of their writing; their papers show more substance than those of their noncommunity peers.

Questions Focus

In a questions-focused evaluation, the first step is to generate a question or questions to which the answer will make a real difference in terms of program development and what students and teachers experience in learning communities. The questions need to be shaped by program stakeholders and should recognize local contexts and meaning. Patton (1997), citing Le Guin, stresses that "how one poses a question frames the answer one gets–and its utility" (p. 185).

A 1998–1999 study of learning communities at the University of Michigan was designed to assess "whether several different learning communities of varying types and purposes on the same campus can contribute both individually and cumulatively to improve students' outcomes" (Kurotsuchi Inkelas, 1999, p. 2); or, "how [do] different types of living-learning programs foster differential student outcomes?" (p. 40). The study would yield answers that could be used at the university level to better understand how various living-learning communities contribute to the educational development of students and by individual programs to help them improve specific aspects of their living-learning community, including services and programs.

The study revealed that students make use of different types of programs to meet different needs. There was an overall improvement in outcomes for students who participated in living-learning programs compared to those who did not participate, but there were also differences in student outcomes among the three types of living-learning programs: four-year academic programs, transition programs, and academic initiative programs. Kurotsuchi Inkelas (1999) concluded that each program achieved in its intended area of focus. "Students in programs designed to assist them in making the transition from home to college indicated that they had the greatest ease with managing new responsibilities, such as money and time management and locating assistance when they needed it" (p. 60). In addition, students in academic programs preferred cognitively advanced activities; this is consistent with these programs' emphases on academic enrichment.

Conclusion

The various approaches or foci of learning communities evaluation and assessment described in this chapter share a common characteristic—the studies were conducted by and for program leadership with a primary goal of program improvement. Collecting information on what participants experience in learning communities is essential not only to improve and sustain learning community programs but also (and perhaps more important) to improve teaching and learning at the individual learning community level. In the early stages of program development, the pressure to advance to Level Five (see Table 6.1), program impact, will be strong. However, it is important to remember that data collected to demonstrate accountability (Jacob's recommended Level Two) can also justify a program's ongoing existence and expansion.

This chapter stressed the importance of local evaluation and assessment. In understanding the true potential of learning communities as a more global model for undergraduate education reform, however, there is a need for larger, institutional assessments of student learning that can be normed or aligned across similar types of institutions so more national standards and models of best practice can be generated. To achieve this goal, the question many learning community programs are already asking on their respective campuses—How are we doing?—may need to be expanded to, How are we doing compared to other, similar programs?

CHAPTER SEVEN

APPROACHING DIVERSITY THROUGH LEARNING COMMUNITIES

Emily Decker Lardner

In the past ten years, our collective understanding of the concept of diversity and its ramifications has blossomed in higher education. Important work has been done through student affairs to bring issues of the presence and absence of historically underrepresented people—as students, faculty, administrators, and staff—into the foreground of all discussions of diversity. Simultaneously, scholars have enriched the work in all disciplines by cultivating knowledge about peoples, practices, cultures, and history. A body of knowledge has also been shaped about pedagogical practices that work with students from underrepresented groups, as well as those that help traditional majority students develop multicultural competencies and awareness of perspectives and histories other than their own. Although diversity can be defined in many ways, the underlying goal of this chapter is to highlight practices that increase the presence and improve the academic success of students of color—in particular, African American students, Latino and Hispanic students, Native American students, and Asian and Pacific Islander students. Research shows that when schools and colleges are designed to facilitate the success of students of color, other students benefit as well.

Educators aligned with learning communities and diversity grapple with an identical question: At what point do the practices cultivated for these particular programs become widespread throughout an institution? At what point does an institution reach its tipping point so that systemic change occurs? In *Transforming the Multicultural Education of Teachers,* Michael Vavrus (2002) argues that successful multicultural educators have learned how to engage the uneasy coexistence of a transformed and a more traditional curriculum within a single school: "Transformative multicultural education pragmatically recognizes and engages this tension as an inherent aspect of meeting multicultural education goals" (p. 7). Likewise, learning community practitioners have come to realize that transformed curricular structures usually coexist with more traditional curricular structures, and the challenge in most institutions is learning how to engage this tension in pragmatic and productive ways. One place to start this work is by purposefully connecting communities of practice—in this case, the communities of practice that have evolved around diversity work and those that have organized around learning communities.

Diversity work on campuses takes many forms, and at their best, learning communities build on this existing work. Learning communities can be designed to invite students from underrepresented groups into the academy and to help them stay and be academically successful. The curriculum developed for learning communities, in its interdisciplinarity and its focus on issues that matter in the world, can readily include multiple worldviews and histories. Learning communities can also become places where teachers develop powerful pedagogical strategies that support the learning of all students. The three central elements for approaching diversity through learning communities are

1. Designing learning communities for particular groups of students
2. Using learning communities as sites for curriculum transformation
3. Developing pedagogical practices that support diverse learners

Reflecting on these three elements is at the core of connecting the widely recognized power of learning community structures with the rich work that has been done around diversity issues over the past two decades.

Designing Learning Communities for Particular Groups of Students

The demographic profile of students involved in postsecondary education in the United States is changing as the overall demographic profile of this country is changing. California, Texas, and New Mexico are on the verge of becoming "minority majority" states (Rendon and Hope, 1996). According to the National Center for Education Statistics (2003), *Digest of Statistics,* in 2000, 28 percent of college students were minorities, compared with 15 percent in 1996. The proportion of white students has decreased, while the proportion of students in each other racial or ethnic group has increased. Much of the change can be attributed to rising numbers of Hispanic and Asian or Pacific Islander students. The proportion of Asian or Pacific Islander students rose from 2 percent to 6 percent, and the Hispanic proportion rose from 4 percent to 10 percent during that period. The proportion of black students fluctuated during most of the early part of the period, before rising slightly to 11 percent in 2000 from 9 percent in 1976. Nonresident aliens for whom race and ethnicity is not reported comprise 4 percent of the total enrollment. (http://nces.ed.gov/pubs2003/digest02/ch_3.asp#1).

Colleges across the country are making efforts to recruit and retain students of color, and many campuses are developing learning communities for that purpose. Tinto (1987) suggests retention is a function of three strategies, all of which can be incorporated into the design of learning communities:

1. Integrating social and academic activities, formally and informally
2. Addressing issues of academic preparedness, making sure that students have the skills they need in order to be academically successful once they are admitted to our campuses
3. Engendering a sense of belonging to a community on campus

Once a campus identifies areas where numbers of students are not succeeding academically, it can design a learning community program as a strategic intervention. The University of Texas in El Paso wanted to improve the success of students of color in its science, math, and engineering programs, so they developed a cluster model of learning communities. Connie Kubo Della Piana describes their learning communities initiative and experience.

Promoting Achievement for Diverse Learners: Learning Communities at the University of Texas in El Paso (Connie Kubo Della Piana)

This case story from the University of Texas-El Paso (UTEP) (Della Piana, 2001) illustrates how learning communities can be purposefully designed to attract and support students of color. UTEP received a National Science Foundation award of about $2.5 million to create learning communities focused on science, math, and engineering for students of color. UTEP's goal is to make sure that students have access to quality science and engineering education. UTEP is a commuter campus with 82 percent of students from El Paso County; 70 percent of UTEP students are Hispanic, and 55 percent are first-generation college students. Although learning community programs are offered to all students, the underlying purpose is to get more Hispanic students into science, math, and engineering programs, retain them at a higher level, and increase graduation rates.

At UTEP, all students who go into science, engineering, and math take a learning community after they have taken a mandatory summer orientation. Incoming students have very high expectations, and one goal for the faculty and staff involved with the learning community program is to make sure that students have the necessary skills to achieve their expectations. These students come from communities in which engineering and law are considered fields where one can make money and have a good career; students enter the university with those goals in mind. The first step in the process, then, is to make sure students understand what they need to succeed.

After orientation, students are placed into learning communities organized around their math placement results. These learning communities include a freshman seminar with a science and engineering orientation, the math course they placed into, and an English course. Faculty teaching the courses are encouraged to use cooperative learning practices. The learning communities include peer facilitators who are upper-division students, many from science and engineering. These learning communities are designed to help students form an academic and social community and to make sure students have opportunities to develop the academic skills they need to be successful—particularly math skills.

In 1997, the retention rate for students in UTEP learning communities was 77 percent, compared with an overall retention rate of 68 percent. Consequently, the program was asked to scale up from around seventy to four hundred entering science, engineering, and math students. The one-year retention rate for this larger group of students was 80 percent, regardless of their math placement. Disaggregated data showed a significant difference in the retention of Hispanic students, and the retention of male and female students approached statistical significance. Student achievement is another goal of the learning community program. Achievement is measured in terms of GPA, and early results suggest that students who have gone through the learning community program have higher GPAs than students who did not.

UTEP's learning community programs were specifically designed to support large numbers of Hispanic students coming to the institution with the intention of entering science, math and engineering. The same kind of analysis of critical needs for students of color will yield different results on other campuses. What the UTEP example demonstrates is that learning communities can become strategic interventions when institutions determine that they want to improve the academic success of students of color in particular parts of the curriculum.

Using Learning Communities as Sites for Curriculum Transformation

Learning communities at UTEP aim to help students develop the knowledge, skills, and abilities required to be successful in math, science, and engineering. The institution's focus on improving student success in math is consistent with broader analyses as well. According to Moses and Cobb (2001), achievement in math is critical to the future of students of color, given the omnipresence of computers and information technology in all parts of economic and social life. The tools that control this technology are based on systems of symbolic representation, and the place where students first encounter this symbolism is in algebra. Moses, founder of The Algebra Project, argues that student success in algebra is the goal around which educators and community members need to organize. The learning community program at UTEP, specifically designed to support the academic achievement of students of color in science, math, and engineering programs, is an example of one such effort.

The Algebra Project also focuses on transforming the curriculum of the standard algebra course, exemplifying a second approach to diversity. Many educators are adopting this approach, which questions the nature of the knowledge and the way it is presented in the curriculum. Transforming the curriculum requires teachers to have a knowledge base "that is responsive to the conditions of people historically placed on the margins of society's political and economic activities" (Vavrus, 2002, p. 18).

The Need for Curriculum Transformation

An incident that occurred at Seattle Central Community College (SCCC) illustrates the power of purposefully designing learning community curriculum to reflect multiple worldviews. Seattle Central launched its first interdisciplinary coordinated studies program (CSP) in 1984. The CSPs were designed as team-taught, interdisciplinary programs organized around themes involving engaging in inquiry, problem solving, identifying issues, and proposing solutions. More than forty CSPs were offered between 1984 and 1989, but student enrollment in the programs did not reflect the multicultural or racial diversity of Seattle Central as a whole. When data from the SCCC research office were analyzed, faculty hypothesized that the college transfer CSPs were not attracting meaningful representation because the themes did not reflect the experiences of multicultural and racially diverse students (Collins and Sheppard, 1989, p. 26). In response, faculty developed a CSP entitled "Our Ways of Knowing: The Black Experience and Social Change," an interdisciplinary learning community linking sociology, literature, and writing as an attempt to connect reality to students' awareness of themselves and their connections in the world (p. 26). Thirty of the forty-nine students who enrolled were African American students, or about 61 percent. (In contrast, only 12 percent of the students enrolled in the previous CSP programs were African American.) As Collins and Sheppard suggest, the design of learning community curriculum presents a rich opportunity for helping students develop a deeper understanding of multiple worldviews and knowledge traditions.

Faculty Development and Curriculum Transformation

Faculty development can be designed to support the development of learning communities as sites for multicultural education. (Faculty development is discussed in Chapter Five.) Ann Intili Morey (1997) suggests that an important foundation for infusing college courses and curricula with content and instructional strategies responsive to our diverse society is the establishment of a learning community among teachers (p. 265). Providing faculty with opportunities to reflect on the goals of their learning communities, goals that affect choice of content and the development of curricular strategies, is key. Reflecting on course goals is one way to begin conversations about potential curriculum transformations.

Margie K. Kitano (1997) lists the kinds of questions about goals that can become the basis for initial conversations. Is the goal to

- Support diverse students' acquisition of traditional subject matter knowledge and skills?
- Help students acquire a more accurate or comprehensive knowledge of subject matter?
- Encourage students to accept themselves or others?
- Understand the history, traditions, and perspectives of specific groups?
- Help students value diversity and equity?
- Equip all students to work actively toward a more democratic society? [p. 19]

Kitano developed a paradigm for multicultural course change that serves a useful tool for faculty conversations. She identified four components of courses—content, instructional strategies and activities, assessment of student knowledge, and classroom dynamics—and describes each component in three developmental stages, from exclusive to inclusive to transformed. For instance, classroom dynamics at an exclusive level tend to focus exclusively on content and avoid social issues. In a transformed environment, classroom dynamics respect rules established for group process and allow students to challenge biased views and share diverse perspectives. In the transformed stage, assessment of student knowledge focuses on student growth, taking the form, for instance, of action-oriented projects, self-assessment, and reflection on the course (p. 24). Critical reflection on the part of teachers is an essential part of the ongoing work of developing multicultural curriculum (Vavrus, 2002). Exhibit 7.1 presents a workshop adapted from "Conceptual Foundations for Social Justice Courses," by Rita Hardiman and Bailey W. Jackson (1997), for faculty teams at the Evergreen State College. The workshop invites faculty into reflective conversations about the nature of their own social identities, their learning community curricula, and the kinds of knowledge (and knowers) it privileges. An important part of the

EXHIBIT 7.1. WHAT DO WE MEAN WHEN WE TALK ABOUT DIVERSITY AND WHAT MIGHT IT MEAN IN PRACTICE?*

One way to think about diversity is to situate ourselves within social groups and social structures within the United States. Each of us has our own practice, our matters of difference and power, and at the same time, we all belong to social groups or are perceived as belonging to social groups that have had more or few systemic privileges relative to other groups. To start this workshop, indicate your own social group memberships.

Social Identities	Membership	Historically powerful?	How comfortable are you talking about issues around this?
Race			
Gender			
Class			
Age			
Sexual orientation			
Religion			
Physical abilities			

1. Talk about your responses with your team. How might your own social identities affect your view of teaching and learning?
2. (30 minutes) How do you imagine working with any differences that have emerged—differences in terms of how you choose to describe yourself, differences in how you feel about even having this conversation, whatever emerges? Within your team, what are your obligations to each other?
3. (30 minutes) Work as a team to conduct your own "environmental" scan about the nature of your curriculum: Who are the authors you've chosen? Whose ideas do they cite? Who are your guest speakers and visitors? What kinds of images are in the materials you have selected? As a team, talk about the obligations you feel toward your disciplines, toward each other, and the content of your program. To what extent does a conversation about diversity enter into your curricular designs? If you vary in your approaches to this question, how are you going to work with each other?
4. (30 minutes) Another way to think about working with differences is to pay attention to pedagogy. A question to consider is this: For each member of your team, what is the nature of your obligation to students? If there are differences among you, how will you work with them?

Source: Kido, Parson, and Decker (2000)

*Adapted from "Conceptual Foundations for Social Justice Courses," by Rita Hardiman and Bailey W. Jackson, in *Teaching for Diversity and Social Justice,* eds. Maurianne Adams, Lee Anne Bell, and Pat Griffin, 1997. Used by permission.

workshop–a place where some teams stopped–is in the first step, which asks faculty to identify their own social identities. Some faculty objected to making this information public among their colleagues; others objected to the phrasing of the question about "historically powerful" even though, in practice, much of the curriculum developed by Evergreen teams transforms traditional structures and sources of knowledge. Nurturing a collective public practice of critical reflection takes time, persistence, and patience, as does the process of curriculum transformation.

Developing Pedagogical Practices That Support Diverse Learners

The *who* and *what* of learning are inextricably linked with the *how* of learning. James Anderson (2001) promotes teaching and assessment practices that facilitate the learning of all students, including those students who have historically not been well served by higher education. He argues that most of the teaching that goes on in higher education is oriented toward learners who tend to be strongly analytical–that is, comfortable learning material in relatively abstract terms or separate from particular contexts, comfortable separating concepts from their own life experiences. As a result, students who tend to be more relationally oriented are often excluded, not through overt discriminatory practices but because the learning environments they find themselves in do not create enough opportunities to connect learning and life or to put new learning into meaningful contexts. Relational learners need more overt cues that the work is worth their while, that their presence is valued, and that useful connections can be made with their own lived experiences.

Much good work has been done to develop pedagogical strategies that support diverse learners by valuing their presence, their voices, and connections with their lived experiences. Critical Moments is one such project. The concept and practice of Critical Moments was developed and piloted in the Goodrich program of the University of Nebraska-Omaha by Diane Gillespie, now an interdisciplinary arts and science faculty member at the University of Washington-Bothell. Critical Moments is used as a retention, awareness, and change project for students of color, other underrepresented students (first-generation college students, students with disabilities, students for whom English is a second language, for example), and the institutions they attend.

At the heart of the project are interviews with students about their "critical moments"–moments when they considered dropping out of college. These interviews become the basis of case stories, which can be discussed by students, faculty, and administrators. Gillies Malnarich (2002), director of the Critical

Moments project based at the Washington Center, observes that "Critical Moments is a particularly powerful complement to the many existing strategies for improving campus climates for diversity and retention because it empowers students to act on behalf of themselves and their communities." Case stories can be used in a variety of educational settings: academic courses, co-curricular organizations, community settings, and staff/faculty development institutes. At some colleges, including the University of Nebraska-Lincoln and Seattle Central Community College, Critical Moments cases form the curricular basis of learning community programs jointly taught by a faculty member and a student affairs professional.

Learning communities create ideal places for faculty and students to develop practices that are inclusive and hospitable. Some strategies, like Critical Moments and a related project known as Intergroup Dialogue (Schoem and Hurtado, 2001), are relatively formal programs rooted in research on teaching, learning, and diversity. Much of the learning about pedagogical strategies that supports diverse learners grows out of years of practice in learning communities, women's studies, ethnic studies, and other courses. As Morey and Kitano (1997) note, the heart of the academic experience—the thing upon which we should continually reflect—is what happens in the classroom, the interactions between teachers and students and the curriculum (p. 10).

The learning community program at LaGuardia Community College incorporates several core practices that promote student engagement and foster the ability of students and faculty to learn together across significant differences. The learning communities programs are thematically based, and the themes are chosen to resonate with students' experiences. Faculty teaching in learning communities meet regularly whether they are team teaching or teaching as part of a cluster. As a result, the learning communities tend to be well integrated, which helps create a stronger community for students. Learning community faculty also develop explicit ground rules for their programs with their students. Phyllis van Slyck and Will Koolsbergen describe their program.

Diversity and Learning Communities at LaGuardia Community College (Phyllis van Slyck and Will Koolsbergen)

LaGuardia Community College stands in the shadow of the United Nations. One of the first things visitors see when they enter the main building on campus is a hall of flags representing every country for which there is a representative at the college (van Slyck and Koolsbergen, 2001). LaGuardia has had learning communities since 1971, beginning with liberal arts clusters, four thematically integrated courses required for liberal arts day students. The college currently offers both college-level and developmental learning communities organized as clusters and pairs and, beginning in 2001, as freshman interest groups (FIGs). Most entering students at LaGuardia test into precollege writing, precollege reading, and precollege math. In 1991, building on the success of the liberal arts clusters, the college developed a new program called the New Student House program, a college within a college for developmental students. The original New Student House consisted of three developmental courses (reading, writing, and speech) and a freshman seminar. Because of financial aid regulations and a change in the credit structure, within two years LaGuardia began to offer New Student House with basic reading, basic writing, freshman seminar, and one college-level course (Oral Communication, Introduction to Business, or Introduction to Computers). The content course is selected to suit students' needs from a developmental perspective but also to support their interests in majors and professions. An ESL (English as a Second Language) version of New Student House is also offered and includes Communication for the non-native speaker as the credit-bearing course. New Student Houses are designed to support a very at-risk population: students requiring one or more developmental courses or assistance in language proficiency. Like the liberal arts clusters, these houses have a highly integrated curriculum, which includes a joint syllabus and shared readings and activities.

Given that the population of students in developmental programs reflects the general student body, in a group of thirty students, probably twenty-five nationalities will be represented. Out of necessity, faculty teaching in the program need to face issues of diversity. New Student House programs are organized around themes, and faculty discovered early that one way to deal with diversity is to give students a voice so that they can tell their stories by picking a theme that resonates for everyone. For example, "relationships" proved to be more fruitful than "work," because not all students had had work experience. What has happened is that the learning community programs have become a place for students to develop oral histories about who and what they are. For several years, these oral histories were transformed into theater pieces. Students were able to tell their stories, and they were able to direct other students in their stories. So students were encouraged not only to give voice to their experiences but also to take charge of the way their stories would be told, from what point of view, and through what form. This opportunity provides a diverse population an environment in which they can feel comfortable enough to tell who and what they are.

One of the very strong features of LaGuardia's learning communities is that they are thematically integrated. Faculty who choose to work in learning communities meet and plan a coordinated curriculum around a specific theme. This integration is reinforced during the semester; faculty in clusters team teach during an integrated hour, and all learning communities faculty meet regularly to review the curriculum, talk about what is working, and change what needs to be changed. Learning communities create something close to an ideal (nothing is ever ideal) opportunity to work with diversity issues because students and faculty in learning communities already have a kind of community. They have more potential to build trust, so difficult issues that need to be talked about can be handled in a safer way.

One important strategy for facilitating conversations in the classroom is the use of ground rules. LaGuardia faculty borrowed the following rules published by Lynn Weber Canon (1990) in *Women's Studies Quarterly* and use them regularly in learning community programs. The ground rules ask students to acknowledge that racism, classism, sexism, heterosexism, and other institutionalized forms of oppression exist and that one mechanism of institutionalized oppression is that we are all systematically misinformed about our own group and members of other groups. Students are asked to agree not to blame others or themselves for misinformation learned and to accept responsibility for not repeating misinformation. They are asked to assume that people always do the best they can, actively combat myths and stereotypes that prohibit group cooperation, and create an atmosphere that is safe for open discussion.

By design, in seminar, students are supposed to be more active participants in the teaching, learning, and classroom management processes. Sometimes seminar instructors introduce ground rules, but more often students are invited to help create them. This is a delicate process. Faculty know the kinds of ground rules that will foster the classroom community, and faculty also know that students need the chance to develop them on their own so that they have some ownership of them. Teachers have to be good enough actors to let the students think that they are creating the rules entirely. Essentially, teachers walk into their classrooms and say, "Look, we're going to talk about some really great things in here. But sometimes we may see things differently, so in order for us to maintain some kind of order in what could be a chaotic democracy, we have to have some basic rules. So what are your ideas, what are some of the rules you think we should follow?" Usually, no one will respond, and so the teacher volunteers an easy one, like "raise your hand to be recognized to speak." Someone writes it on the board, and then the class moves to the next ground rule. The process can take anywhere from fifteen minutes to an hour, depending on class dynamics. It's always an enriching discussion because of etiquette differences across cultures, for example, not showing the bottoms of your feet in class.

Once the list is on the board, the teacher steps back and suggests the class look it over for things to add, to take away, to negotiate. When the list is finalized, the teacher types it up and gives a copy to every student to keep. One copy gets passed around and everyone signs it, like the Declaration of Independence. Some teachers laminate the signed copy and carry it with them to class. The first time a discussion goes awry, the list comes out. After that, students look after the process. If someone fails to raise his or her hand or engages in inappropriate dialogue, students take care of it. They will be very polite at the beginning, but they can become very insistent. After using the rules for two or three weeks, students do a two-minute essay on their reactions to how they are being used. That gives the teacher a chance to facilitate any necessary changes. All of this attention to process takes time, but it supports the development of a community of learners. From a more academic point of view, it also helps students apply critical thinking and critical reflection skills to the classroom dynamic and their own roles within that dynamic. Sometimes when students leave the class, teachers will give them the rules on a small, laminated card and encourage their use in other classes.

Ground rules work in an electronic classroom as well as in person. At LaGuardia, ground rules are also used in FIG seminars, which are held in a computer lab. The seminars are led by "master learners," senior faculty members or administrators of the college. Students in the FIG seminar are learning a program called "Speakeasy," which is very user-friendly. The software lets faculty set up discussion boards for students and post assignments, while students can read and respond to each other's work. Ground rules may be posted on-screen so they're always visible.

Integrating the Who, the What, and the How: The Case for "Multicontextuality"

In *Beyond Affirmative Action: Reframing the Context for Higher Education*, Robert Ibarra (2001) argues that for American higher education to make good on the promise of access and equity, incremental change—including the development of learning communities—is not enough. We need a new conceptual framework. Until now, Ibarra argues, diversity efforts have been grounded in the pipeline metaphor that emerged after the Civil Rights Act of 1964, when the first diversity programs in the country were organized to create better access for "educationally disadvantaged populations." Ibarra argues that the mission of early diversity programs was fourfold:

1. Increase the number of minority students on campus through selective recruiting.
2. Offer academic support for underprepared minority students, which evolved into other academic support programs, including orientations, writing workshops, study skills workshops, and ESL support units.
3. Assist in meeting the financial needs of minority students through scholarships.
4. Offer academic advice and counseling, particularly from trained minority staff [p. 236].

When these programs were first implemented, they were very successful largely because there were few minority students on campuses. Ibarra (2001) argues that these early programs focused on a symptom—the lack of presence of minority students—rather than on a more fundamental problem in the higher education system. After nearly forty years of trying to "fix" the problem of the lack of presence of minority students and faculty, the real problem facing higher education and educational activists has become more apparent. According to Ibarra, "Academic culture has always been the central problem for ethnic minorities in higher education. The difference is that today we must rethink and reframe the operative paradigm to address the real problem, which is academic organizational cultures that prefer to confront, not collaborate. And in no way are the pipeline programs born in the 1960s capable of dealing with the growing problem of high-context, field-sensitive students who are abandoning (or never entering) graduate schools, which are dominated by low-context, field-independent professors" (p. 243). In response to the problem of academic culture, Ibarra argues that the culture of higher education needs to change in order to support learners who are diverse in terms of both context and cognition.

Ibarra grounds his discussion of context in the work of Edward and Mildred Hall, who distinguish between high- and low-context cultures. Individuals from high-context cultures "tend to use the multiple streams of information that surround an event, situation, or interaction (e.g., words, tones, gestures, body language, status or relationship of speakers) to determine meaning from the context in which it occurs" (p. 53). Individuals from low-context cultures typically do the opposite by filtering out the conditions surrounding an event or interaction and focusing primarily on the words. Higher education is predominantly a low-context culture. Another characterization of the culture of academe is that it is biased toward field-independent individuals, those who tend to do well in impersonal environments. In contrast, field-sensitive individuals learn best when those in authority express confidence in their ability to do well and from materials that have human, social content (p. 56). Ibarra's theory of multicontextuality, which he characterizes as an adaptive strategy exercised by individuals, helps suggest the kind of academic culture we need to create in order to support diverse learners.

Because of their emphasis on community and integrative learning, learning communities are critical sites for practicing multicontextuality. As the following case story illustrates, robust learning community programs can incorporate a range of practices that support multicontextual learners. The Evergreen State College-Tacoma program was intentionally designed to serve a particular population of students. After it was started, analysis of student needs led to the development of a partnership with a neighboring community college to help students get through all four years of college. In addition, the curriculum of the Evergreen State College-Tacoma (TESC-Tacoma) program reflects elements of students' lived experiences, and by running parallel day and evening programs, the learning community program makes it easy for students to make up classes. The program is structured as a cluster model, which allows students to develop their own major interests, and it includes a weekly integrative seminar taught by faculty, plus an all-program lecture, ensuring that students develop a range of relationships. All members of the learning community—students, faculty, and staff—are expected to practice the four core values articulated for the program as a whole. The design of the physical space encourages frequent, informal interaction among students and faculty. Joye Hardiman presents the TESC-Tacoma story.

Multicontextuality in Practice: The Evergreen State College-Tacoma Campus (Joye Hardiman)

The Evergreen State College was founded as an alternative public liberal arts college organized through a series of team-taught, thematically organized, interdisciplinary programs—learning communities (Hardiman, 2001). The Evergreen State College-Tacoma campus was developed to meet the needs of working adults who were interested in having access to this form of education in their own community. As a result, the campus population has grown from four women who studied together around the campus founder's kitchen table to a cohort of over two hundred students with their own building. The program was "brought into the center of the institution" in 1984 as an upper-division program. The founder insisted that the program not be marginalized, that its operation monies be embedded within the academic budget to protect it from budget cuts.

Soon it became clear that many community members lacked the first ninety credits of a degree, so Evergreen developed an articulation agreement with Tacoma Community College (TCC), and TCC now offers a "bridge" program on the Evergreen-Tacoma campus. Eighty four percent of TCC Bridge students go on to complete four-year degrees from Evergreen. The retention and graduation rate in the upper-division program fluctuates between 91 and 95 percent. The Evergreen-Tacoma student population includes 40 percent African American, 39 percent European American, 8 percent Hispanic, 4 percent Asian American, 5 percent Native American, and 4 percent international. One hundred percent are commuters. The campus has success with these students because it is contextually responsive, value based, and philosophically and physically structured to promote student success and excellence.

The class schedule is contextually friendly. The curriculum is organized so the same courses offered during the day are offered again in the evening. If a student has to miss a class due to a sick baby or a change in work schedule, he or she has the option of attending the other class. The program content is organized so information given in Tuesday's all-program assembly can be used in seminars on Wednesday and shared in the barber and beauty shops on Saturday. When they enter, students are asked what they want to do when they graduate. The expectation of success is built in from this welcoming ritual to the course requirements, including those courses that have traditionally been roadblocks for marginalized people but are critical for success in graduate school or community leadership.

The Evergreen-Tacoma curriculum is based on students' needs, community realities, and faculty passion. All students must write an autobiography in which they explore the lessons learned and the wisdom earned by living their lives. They have to demonstrate skills in statistics, quantitative and qualitative research methodology, and computer and multimedia technology and must complete a senior synthesis detailing their intellectual journey up to the point of college graduation. Most assignments are collaborative, and many involve family or work in the student's own communities. Applause occurs frequently, and people are publicly praised for their accomplishments. An inclusive curriculum is attempted by consciously selecting books and issues that reflect the histories and cultures of students who enroll, as well as addressing issues that matter to the wider community. Each spring, all-program collaborative projects occur through which students take their theoretical work out into the community and make a difference in some way. Student projects have included advocacy work with the homeless, domestic violence survivors, schools, environmental justice groups, citizen advisory boards, the courts, juvenile authorities, arts organizations, cultural and ethnic communities, and nonprofit groups and foundations. Students also work with younger students through instructing, mentoring, and facilitating an Intel Computer Clubhouse.

The campus is very intentional in terms of its value system. The entry hall says "enter to learn, depart to serve," a motto adapted from Bethune Cookman College, a historically black college in Florida. Four core values—inclusivity, reciprocity, hospitality, and civility—guide campus interactions and curriculum. Inclusivity and reciprocity are practiced in the design of the curriculum. Hospitality is practiced by the expectation that multiple members of the community will greet everyone who walks into the building respectfully and cordially. Civility is an expected norm and the key to creating a cohesive community. Conflicts are managed through a social contract and procedural chain.

Indigenous learning structures were taken into consideration when designing the new campus. Courtyards and circles were found at the center of traditional learning spaces and community hearts. So in the new facility, visitors walk into an open commons with faculty offices along two sides. Because the campus didn't want a division between the faculty and the students, the offices are made of glass, creating a learning "market," like the Marrakesh market or the 125th street market in Harlem. In the morning, the faculty slide open their wooden doors, which means they are open for learning business, and when they do private work they slide the doors closed. The commons includes a living room–like arrangement of couches and overstuffed chairs plus a space with tables and chairs for conversations and shared meals, both critical elements on a commuter campus. On the second floor of the new building are four learning labs: an urban environmental science and public health lab, a computer research lab, a multimedia lab, and a civics and democracy lab designed like a moot court, where students practice debating and discussing policy issues. The Tacoma campus has worked very hard to merge learning community work and diversity work in terms of students, curriculum, campus core values, and physical space (Hardiman, 2001).

Conclusion: Challenges for Practitioners

This decade is likely to be characterized by national, state, and local struggles about the appropriate balance between private gains and public good. Critical markers of this conversation will be decisions made locally, at the state level, and nationally about the collection and subsequent allocation of resources. The public good, like accessible and equitable education for all, will be weighed against individual gains in the form of taxes. In the face of an economic decline, with more uncertainty in sight, colleges and universities are deciding which programs to keep, which to cut, what kinds of services comprise core missions, what can be removed. The climate is ripe for directors and advocates of historically marginal programs—learning communities and diversity programs—to be pitted against each other in the competition for increasingly scarce resources.

Ironically, the two efforts can support each other. Learning communities represent a powerful strategy for supporting learners from diverse backgrounds. Because learning communities are frequently interdisciplinary in nature, they can be designed to tackle problems faced by people in the world and draw from the rich intellectual and artistic legacies of people around the world. As an education reform effort, learning communities deserve attention and advocacy; they can present rich opportunities for significant learning for all students.

To realize the dream in this country of widespread access to and significant achievement in postsecondary education, practitioners with expertise in learning communities and in diversity must find ways to connect their practices, form their own learning community focused on designing communities for particular students, transform the curriculum to make it more inclusive, and develop the pedagogical practices that lead to substantive learning for all students. Forming alliances with educators who share commitments to making higher education accessible and hospitable for students of color and other historically marginalized groups is critical to this work, even when the practice of those commitments takes different forms. Patience and persistence and a willingness to learn from the experiences of others will help communities of educators continue to discover not only the implications of their own social identities for their work but also how learning communities can be designed and implemented to support the learning of all.

CHAPTER EIGHT

SUSTAINING LIVING-LEARNING PROGRAMS

David Schoem

Living-learning programs represent two central ideals in higher education: learning and community. Although they clearly fit as a subset within the broader definition and parameters of learning communities, living-learning programs have a distinctive and noteworthy history and tradition of their own. Also known as residential learning communities or residential colleges, living-learning programs are characterized by scholarly community, deep learning, strong sense of community, the careful integration of the intellectual and social dimensions of university life, and democratic education with a spirit of innovation and experimentation (Meiklejohn, 1932; Goodman, 1964; Newmann and Oliver, 1967; Boyer, 1987; Guarasci and Cornwell, 1997). In this chapter, living-learning programs are defined broadly as programs organized to introduce and integrate academic and social learning in residence hall settings through faculty involvement with the goal of an enriched learning experience for all participants.

The chapter begins with a discussion of the characteristics of living-learning programs, followed by definitions of three distinctive models of living-learning programs: residential colleges, residential learning communities, and residential education programs. The three models are then organized into a typology of living-learning programs that describes the common characteristics of each approach. Discussion of the unique challenges involved in creating, improving, and sustaining living-learning programs follows. Located throughout the chapter are snapshots of living-learning programs that are models of success. Each of these snapshots, provided and written by their program leaders, offers a brief description of the program, key challenges they have faced, and the most salient points of their sustainability. The chapter concludes with some of the generalizable lessons culled from the experiences of these living-learning programs.

The Educational Promise of Living-Learning Programs

Living-learning programs are often recognized for their rich learning, innovative teaching, enduring sense of community, and the personally transforming experience they provide for many students and their teachers. These programs, however, often face significant institutional challenges, and their continued viability on any given campus is an ongoing concern from year to year. Yet today, the structural complexities that are a feature of every college and university, the sense of impersonality at many larger universities, and the failure on most campuses to fully tap into the rich intellectual potential of bringing our students and faculty together call for a renewal and strengthening of the bold vision represented by living-learning programs. At their best, living-learning programs represent the genuine model of learning and community (Ryan, 2001; Waltzer, 1992) that is so much desired but still so elusive at many of our colleges and universities.

The Scholarly Community

Living-learning programs provide a structure for realizing the ideal of the scholarly community (Waltzer, 1992; Smith, 1992; Ryan, 1992). They provide a setting for faculty and students to come together to explore ideas across disciplinary boundaries and beyond the limitations of classroom meeting times. They open doors for intellectual creativity and pedagogical innovation, and they provide opportunities for reflection, inquiry, and discovery. In living-learning programs, students are recognized and respected as emerging scholars and are given voice to express ideas and opinions. Ideas are linked to social problems, and students are involved in real-world communities and their concerns. Faculty in living-learning programs can pursue their scholarship in a supportive academic community.

Deep Learning

Living-learning programs offer an opportunity for learning to go well beyond the boundaries of the classroom into people's lives (Astin, 1993). By virtue of the fact that students who study together in classes also live together in the same residence halls, they provide a natural setting for students to take ideas and concepts from the classroom out into the world. The residence hall environment becomes a twenty-four-hour-a-day setting for intellectual engagement. Students continue stimulating discussions from their small classes into the cafeteria, along hallway corridors late into the night, out into community service project sites, and onto the athletic playing field. Students find it easy and valuable to collaborate in study groups, group projects, and in discussions of intriguing books and ideas. The meaning of college learning is transformed for students from a never-ending series of lectures, exams, quizzes, papers, and grades to a core component of one's identity, discussions, creativity, discovery, values, relationships, community, worldview, and life and professional choices.

Snapshots of Successful Programs: University of Maryland at College Park, College Park Scholars (Kathy McAdams, Kevin Baxter, http://www.scholars.umd.edu)

College Park Scholars admitted its first class of 250 students in 1994. Today, the program regularly admits 915 students (about 22 percent of the freshman class) into its twelve programs. The faculty and staff number nearly fifty, and facility development is nearly complete. The program offers thirty to forty courses in a given semester. Students take an average of one to four credits per semester with other Scholars' students, similar to that of a curricular minor for freshmen and sophomores. Academic affairs funds the twelve programs, the central administration salaries, and faculty release time. Student affairs supports the resident life staff, the facilities upkeep, the Cambridge Community Center, and the office space in the community.

Key Challenges

College Park Scholars has overcome many challenges. At the top of this list is having twelve different programs under the canopy of College Park Scholars. These programs are supported to different degrees by their sponsoring colleges. This creates an imbalance in their resources and in the numbers of students in any given program. Another challenge has been adjusting to the growing class sizes (250 in 1994; 915 in 2001). The central staff has struggled to keep up and maintain a solid product each year. The divide between students who are in Scholars and those who are not is another challenge. Students in Scholars, like other academic enrichment programs, are provided with various opportunities for experiential learning, whereas others in the general population are not provided with such opportunities.

Points of Sustainability

The true sustainability of College Park Scholars can be attributed to the dedicated faculty and staff that have helped build the community to where it is today. These individuals are the reason for the continued success of the program. College Park Scholars is a vehicle for university recruitment, retention, and residential placement. The program has seen the academic profile of our students rise exponentially. This level of success is due to campus support (in the form of financial resources, faculty release time, college support of individual Scholars programs), facilities improvement, and dedicated faculty and staff. This support is due in part to a revised strategic plan that emphasized the improvement of undergraduate education.

Strong Sense of Community

Living-learning programs model community ideals (Klein, 2000; Eaton, Mac-Gregor, and Schoem, 2003; Parks Daloz, Keen, Keen, and Daloz Parks, 1996). For students, the residence hall setting releases all time constraints on community building and intensifies the experience of living with others. It offers the opposite of the more typical college experience in which one sees a classmate or a professor for a single hour a few times a week and then returns to his or her separate life. Unlike any other time in one's life, on residential campuses students are together constantly for classes, meals, study time, educational programs, and when staying up together very late into the night.

Students in living-learning programs also have the opportunity to construct an environment that addresses the most important elements of community. They live with a diverse group of students from backgrounds different from their own. They must set standards for behavior, and they must regulate and manage conflicts that arise. It is a unique experience of living and practicing democracy.

Faculty members are an integral part of the life of the community. Their presence transforms the environment from a social boot camp for undergraduates to one in which ideas set the context and parameters for living standards. In the living-learning program, faculty scholars are present in the residence hall as teachers, guests, and participants who bring scholarly theory and literature into the lives of students. In the process of building a scholarly community, faculty call upon both theory and practice for standards of living, ethics in relationships, and dialogue in intergroup relations.

Snapshots of Successful Programs: University of Wisconsin-Madison—Bradley Learning Community (Aaron Brower, http://www.housing.wisc.edu/bradley/)

Bradley Learning Community, begun in 1995, has 240 coed freshman students. There are one faculty director, two housing staff, and ten to twelve "faculty fellows" (regular faculty in a variety of departments or schools) who volunteer one to five hours per week to various programs or activities. There are fourteen "peer mentors" (former Bradley students who are now sophomores) in different leadership roles. The overall goals are the integration of in-class and out-of-class learning and enhanced "engagement" with campus. The program provides a one-credit core course for the entire building that is not required, but about 95 percent of students take it. In addition, other courses or sections each semester are reserved for Bradley students (about ten to twelve per semester). The connections with, and support from, student affairs and academic affairs varies among the living-learning programs at UW-Madison. Almost everyone now views these programs as mainstream. They affect many other units and operations, including course registration, summer orientation, admissions, and housing procedures. Each year, about 1,400 students live in one of the five living-learning communities on campus.

Key Challenges

The administrative structure and support varies for each living-learning community. On the positive side, that has created support well-suited to each community. This decentralization also creates some challenges for how student affairs and academic affairs work together. As the university addresses this new model of collaboration, the provost and vice-chancellor for student affairs have begun to find ways for their offices to work together (for example, developing ways for faculty to receive teaching credit for their work in the living-learning communities).

Points of Sustainability

The living-learning programs at Madison have become a recruiting tool and a source of pride for the university. What has helped sustain Bradley and UW-Madison's other living-learning communities is the dedication and commitment of current faculty and staff. Public acknowledgment and publicity associated with local news stories have been important sources of sustainability. The chancellor and UW system president have touted these programs and publicly acknowledged the work of the faculty and staff involved. Such public thank-yous are very valuable.

Academic and Social Integration

The ideal of looking at the student as a whole person, not just focusing on the student's intellectual development in the classroom while leaving aside their social and emotional growth, is a powerful proposition (Dustin and Murchinson, 1993; Kuh, 1996; Schroeder, Minor, and Tarkow, 1999). Alexander Meiklejohn wrote in 1932:

> One of the most urgent needs of the American college—one might almost say "a desperately urgent need"—is that of fusing together the intellectual and social activities of the students. . . . If the whole group is engaged in the same attempt

at learning, then every aspect of the social living becomes steeped in the common purpose. Men breathe it in, eat it in, play it in, smoke it in, study it in, laugh it in, discuss it in, until education becomes what it ought to be—not a set of imposed, demanded, external tasks, but a form of human living and association, the natural and inevitable growth of a healthy organism in a congenial environment [Nelson, 2001, p. 152].

In 1962, noted social psychologist Theodore Newcomb spoke to the dean and executive committee of the liberal arts college at the University of Michigan of his concern that "the lives of Michigan undergraduates were being unhappily divided into two separate and unrelated experiences; the academic world of classroom, laboratory and library, in contrast to the social world of the residence hall or other living arrangement on the periphery of the campus." The university recognized that "experiences outside the classroom, on the fringe of the academic world, become powerful agents of change, be they for good or ill. Though the University has sought—even aggressively—to reach students' minds in the classroom, it has rarely entered the social world of students other than in a mildly regulatory role" (Wunsch, 1966, pp. 1–3). In response, Michigan opened its first living-learning program that year, called the Pilot Program, which later was to become the Residential College.

Snapshots of Successful Programs: University of Michigan— The Residential College (RC) (Charles Bright, Thomas Weisskopf, www.rc.lsa.umich.edu)

The Residential College began in 1967 and currently has about thirty-five faculty full-time equivalent (FTE), an incoming class of about 250 each year, and about 900 students overall. It offers a broad range of courses at all levels and is supported by academic affairs. The distinctive educational mission of the Residential College is to enable students to develop their intellectual interests and creative talents in an environment in which they can find their own voice and relate learning with doing. The RC faculty and staff challenge students to take the initiative in shaping their education, participate actively in classes and extracurricular programs, think critically about what they are learning and reflectively about what they are doing, and engage with the university community as well as the outside world.

Key Challenges

The key challenge, ultimately, is to overcome the tendency for staff in living-learning units to become marginalized, to be seen as ancillary (and subordinate) to the "real" tasks of the university. In the RC's case, it's the issue of lecturers who staff most of the language and arts courses. Underneath this, of course, is the tension within any unit committed to teaching undergraduates in an institutional setting in which most rewards are derived from research and graduate teaching. This has often made it difficult to recruit and retain College of Literature, Science, and the Arts (LSA) faculty involvement in the RC curriculum—and the result has been a reliance on lecturers, most of whom chose the RC because they were committed to its work. This composition of the faculty has contributed to the low esteem of the RC staff members and the condescension they sometimes experience from LSA colleagues. Although people often praise the RC educational program, many also add that the RC is doing this fine job with the "wrong" people.

Points of Sustainability

The fact that it was established as a four-year college, with its own faculty, has had something to do with its sustainability. From the start, the RC was able to build sustained relations with students over their entire undergraduate career. In addition, the RC sustained itself because it is not theme-based. Early on, it established a core curriculum in basic courses (writing, foreign languages, and the arts) that remain central to any liberal arts education and can be adapted to changing student interests and academic "themes." Finally, the RC survives in part because it is not "freestanding." It is because it is a liberal arts curriculum, grounded in a living-learning program and embedded in the larger university, that the RC can combine the intellectual vitality of a small college with the resources of a large research institution, thus giving it the flexibility and its students the array of options that has enabled it to survive.

Learning is rarely an isolated process; it most often occurs in the interactions between faculty and student, in the space between the theoretical and personal, between the mind and the soul. When students read literature, they look within themselves and in the society around them to explore the meaning of the text. When students encounter their peers from different racial, religious, and economic backgrounds, they come face-to-face with social scientific empiricism and theory. When students face a serious illness of friends or family, go rock climbing in a state park, or look at the stars at night, their studies in the natural sciences hold new meaning. The educational programs that students attend outside of class, the clubs they join, the academic advising and career counseling sessions in which they participate, the friendships they form—it is in these moments when intellectual work coheres into a critical life perspective. These experiences allow the student to become a liberally educated and well-rounded person, not just a good test taker or a good memorizer of facts and figures.

Democratic Education and Instructional Innovation

The concept of the living-learning program is rooted in democratic education (Guarasci and Cornwell, 1997; Schoem and Hurtado, 2001; Schoem, 2002; Eaton, MacGregor, and Schoem, 2003; Mallory and Thomas, 2003) with a belief in democratic processes and student leadership and a high tolerance for intellectual risk and social experimentation. Living-learning communities are places of learning that trust students as young scholars and adults, anticipate that faculty will learn from students just as students learn from faculty, and acknowledge that involvement in community and experiential activities all enhance the learning process. Innovative teaching, shared governance, creativity, independence, and collaboration are cherished values. Guarasci and Cornwell (1997) write: "If ever undergraduate education needed a pedagogical model that recombined learning and life inside and outside the classroom, it is at this juncture in college history. Reconnecting the intellectual life with the social and communal development of students is now more than a luxury; it is an imperative for any undergraduate institution that takes seriously its larger obligations to this society and to the full development of its students" (p. 13).

Alexander Meiklejohn (1932; Nelson, 2001) maintained throughout his life that "the true purpose of liberal democratic education was to teach citizens, all citizens, how to deliberate reasonably and cooperatively about issues of common public concern. So far as minds are concerned, the art of democracy is the art of thinking independently together" (p. 331). He believed that the way to teach freedom democratically was to persuade students to believe in their own capacity to teach themselves. Living-learning programs create this type of teaching and learning environment for students.

Snapshots of Successful Programs: Indiana University— Collins Living-Learning Program (Carl Ziegler, http://www.indiana.edu/~llc/)

The Ralph L. Collins Living-Learning Center (LLC) was founded in 1972 and houses approximately four hundred students. The five-person Living-Learning Center staff includes the director, academic coordinator, arts coordinator, promotions/alumni coordinator, and office manager. Each semester, seven to eight instructors teach Collins seminars and service-learning courses. These are usually either regular university faculty or advanced graduate students. The entire LLC budget is under the aegis of the College of Arts and Sciences. The program collects a $100 per-semester fee from each resident to support student programming.

The key philosophy on which the LLC is founded is that college students are capable of taking responsibility for their own education. This is played out in the Collins course development process carried out by the Board of Education Programming, the only such student board in the nation that participates in the creation of fully accredited university courses. It is exemplified by student-initiated programs that include lectures, workshops, and performances by guest scholars and artists. Under the gentle guidance of the staff, the residents run the LLC.

Key Challenges

The amount of time devoted by the director to interacting with applicants and residents is monumental, but experience has shown that this investment pays off handsomely in the long run in terms of the quality of applicants we attract and the residents we retain. Maintaining good lines of communication with all relevant college and university offices is an ongoing concern. It is also a time-consuming and demanding task to keep all relevant college and university offices informed about programs—both academic and extracurricular—offered at the LLC.

Points of Sustainability

- The quality of our programming, including the development of more than five hundred student-developed courses over our thirty-year history
- The dedication of our staff, including the length of term of the directors: the LLC has had only three directors in thirty years
- Real (not symbolic) opportunities for student leadership and planning
- Personal contact with each applicant by the director and approximately 50 percent retention of our residents from year to year
- A very good working relationship with the office of Residential Programs and Services and a single physical location
- The ability to demonstrate consistently to the university that a residential unit of the college can contribute valuable academic diversity to the curriculum
- Control of our own budget

Definitions and Typology of Living-Learning Programs

The umbrella category of "living-learning programs" encompasses a great many educational initiatives based in varying degrees upon the collegiate ideals discussed earlier. Regardless of their organization, purposes, or degree of success, living-learning programs share common characteristics. Although there is great variation and overlap in the different types of living-learning programs, three distinctive models stand out: residential colleges, residential learning communities, and residential education programs. Although these categories represent distinct types, it is often the case that individual programs label themselves without regard to the distinctiveness of each category. This practice can sometimes add considerable confusion as to what any given program represents in terms of educational philosophy or practice.

Some living-learning programs are four-year, degree-granting colleges (or clusters) within a larger college or university; some are first-year transitional programs with faculty and courses; and others are educationally enhanced residence halls with no courses and minimal faculty involvement. In some cases, programs represent a high degree of integration and sharing of resources and philosophy between academic affairs and student affairs. In other cases, the programs lay fully within the domain of either academic or student affairs. Some living-learning programs are comprehensive liberal arts programs, whereas others focus on a specific disciplinary or preprofessional area, an intellectual theme, an activity, or a specific demographic constituency.

Some institutions feature more than one type of living-learning program. At Iowa State University (http://www.iastate.edu/~learncommunity) and the University of Missouri at Columbia (http://www.missouri.edu/~figwww), variations of two models of living-learning programs exist. At the University of Michigan (www.lsa.umich.edu/mlc), all three models are in place in different programs. All of these different models of living-learning programs can be beneficial for students. With so much variation, it is important for colleges and universities to realistically describe their programs and to note the important distinctions of each type and their implications for learning, practice, and structure.

The Residential College

The residential college dates back to the Oxford Residential Colleges in England (www.ox.ac.uk/aboutoxford/unicol.shtml) and later in the United States to Harvard (www.college.harvard.edu/student/houses), Yale (www.yale.edu/living/colleges.html), University of California-Santa Cruz (http://www2.ucsc.edu/cowell/about_cowell/about_cowell.html), James Madison College at Michigan State University (www.jmc.msu.edu/stafflist.asp), and the University of Miami (http://www.miami.edu/student/housing). Smith (1992) writes that "A residential college is ideally characterized by faculty and students living, studying, and socializing under the same roof. In some programs, faculty are heavily invested (teaching, advising, taking meals) but don't live in residence. In others, faculty live-in, but do little with students."

Mark Ryan (2001) outlines six goals that help conceptualize the residential college, including (1) ethics, (2) citizenship, (3) community, (4) instruction,

(5) co-curricular programming, and (6) peer learning. He places these goals within Smith's broader context of "faculty and students sharing living and working space" (p. 60). In the United States, the term *residential colleges* encompasses a broad spectrum of programs and activities. Robert O'Hara of the University of North Carolina at Greensboro developed a website dedicated to residential colleges within the living-learning program umbrella (http://collegiateway.org/). The following definition attempts to capture the range of residential college programs: a multiyear residential academic program, sometimes degree granting or offering an academic concentration, whose primary feature is that it provides substantial faculty involvement with students through one or more means such as courses, tutorials, advising, or live-in arrangements.

The Residential Learning Community

Curricular learning communities are structures that link courses, integrate the curriculum, organize faculty and students into smaller groups, and help students establish academic and social networks (Shapiro and Levine, 1999; Gabelnick, MacGregor, Matthews, and Smith, 1990). Residential living-learning communities combine the characteristics of curricular learning communities with the ideals of living-learning programs. Residential living-learning communities are one-year or multiyear residential academic programs, with dedicated faculty and a set of courses that are linked together in any one of a variety of curricular structures. These courses are often held in the residence hall, where faculty members also maintain offices. The Michigan Community Scholars Program at the University of Michigan (www.lsa.umich.edu/mcs), Deciding Student Wing at Temple University (www.temple.edu/university_studies/dsw.html), and a number of the programs at Iowa State University (http://www.iastate.edu/~learncommunity) fit this model.

The Residential Education Program

Many living-learning programs are not residential colleges but also do not fit the curricular learning communities framework. These programs are best characterized by their co-curricular nature and structures that meaningfully extend learning into student living space. Activities might include a program that brings students together around a common interest and brings faculty into the residence hall, usually on a onetime basis, for discussions, lectures, films, mentoring, or receptions. Various definitions have been proposed to describe this type of program. The Residential Learning Communities International Clearinghouse (http://www.bgsu.edu/colleges/as/clc/rlcch/index.html), sponsored by Bowling Green State University, uses the following definition: "a residential education unit in a college or university that is organized on the basis of an academic theme or approach and is intended to integrate academic learning and community living." Examples of this model include the Academic and Language Theme Houses at Stanford University (http://rescomp2.stanford.edu/resed), the Academic Center at UC Berkeley (www.reshall.berkeley.edu/academics/), and the Living/Learning Center at San Diego State University (http://www.sa.sdsu.edu/src/fsp/FSP_home.html). A working definition of residential education programs that expands on the clearinghouse definition and encompasses the wide range of programs in this category is the following: a one- or two-year program, usually initiated by student affairs or its housing division, but sometimes with support from or in collaboration with an academic unit, that involves an intentional and cohesive educational focus for students that goes beyond what typically characterizes the traditional residence hall.

Table 8.1 lays out common characteristics across the three categories of living-learning programs. The typology indicates common (C) and uncommon (U) characteristics by program type. While the typology reflects the most typical practices across program type, for some programs the characterizations will not perfectly match their structure or activities.

The Challenges of Building and Supporting Living-Learning Programs

In planning and sustaining living-learning programs, there are many difficult challenges, many unique to living-learning programs that must be understood and addressed. Recognizing these challenges early on may help a campus negotiate and overcome potential obstacles to sustaining a living-learning program. Common challenges faced by living-learning programs include cross-campus partnerships, administrative and budgetary support, faculty involvement, sustained leadership, diversity, student engagement and community building, assessment, and risk taking and innovation.

Cross-Campus Partnerships

Complex institutional relationships pose the greatest obstacle to living-learning programs. Because these programs cross so many institutional boundaries and often depend on the support and resources of other units, these relationships are of central concern. Typically, levels of support and goodwill for any single program vary considerably over time and depend on the leadership in different units, shifting institutional priorities, and changes in the financial landscape. These delicate relationships exist both within and across units, depending on the type of living-learning program.

TABLE 8.1. TYPOLOGY OF LIVING-LEARNING PROGRAMS

Program Type	Residential College	Residential Learning Community	Residential Education
Program Length			
Four-year (may be degree granting)	C	U	U
Multiyear program	C	C	C
First-year transition program	U	C	C
Faculty Involvement			
Faculty live-in residence hall	C	U	U
Graduate instructors live-in	C	C	U
Faculty appointment (assigned to the program)	C	C	U
Faculty appointment is on a temporary/adjunct basis	C	C	C
Classes in residence hall	C	C	U
Faculty offices in residence hall	C	C	U
Faculty participate in co-curricular educational programs	C	C	C
Courses/Curriculum			
Comprehensive curriculum	C	U	U
First-year seminars	C	C	U
Writing courses	C	C	U
Discipline-specific courses	C	C	U
Interdisciplinary offerings	C	C	U
Various forms of linked courses (links, FIGs, clusters, coordinated studies)	C	C	U
Nonlinked recitations sections of campus courses	C	C	C
University "101"/freshman seminar courses	C	C	C
Sponsorship/Leadership			
Academic and student affairs shared collaboration	U	C	C
Academic affairs primary or only	C	C	U
Student affairs (housing) primary or only	U	U	C

Program Type	Residential College	Residential Learning Community	Residential Education
Focus and Activities			
Liberal Arts	C	C	U
Theme-based (Diverse Democracy, Health Sciences, Environment)	U	C	C
Common activity (research, community service, arts)	U	C	C
Targeted group of students (gender, race, ethnicity)	U	C	C
Academic status (honors, academic support)	C	C	U
Student leadership	C	C	C
Academic advising within the program	C	U	U
Academic support services	C	C	C
Students dine together	C	C	C
Intramural athletic teams	C	U	U

The relationship between academic affairs and student affairs is critical to the success of the program. The partnership needs to be based on shared educational goals. Long-standing institutional divisions exist between academic affairs and student affairs (Schroeder and Hurst, 1996; Rong, 1998). It is the exception to find a relationship of collaboration, respect, and trust between the different units, yet that is precisely what is necessary for living-learning programs to thrive.

Sometimes, even in settings in which good cooperation and collaboration exist, the fact that the two units operate within different organizational structures can cause problems. Issues arise over control and responsibility for remodeling and renovating the physical space, planning and teaching calendars, staff development, budget preparation, hiring and evaluation procedures, even language and terminology. Few faculty have entered a residence hall since their college days or even know that a student affairs unit exists on campus, and most student affairs staff have not recently been to a faculty office or classroom and have little concrete idea what constitutes the life of a departmental faculty member.

Some universities attempt to work around such divisions, rather than addressing them directly, by creating programs solely within the domain of either academic or student affairs, thus giving them a single funding source. Too often these programs miss the inherent opportunity of living-learning programs to join the academic and social experiences of students. Rather than providing the "seamless interweaving" of the academic and social dimensions of the undergraduate experience, this approach offers structured "visitations" between academic and student affairs. When a faculty member comes into a residence hall for a onetime fireside chat, that person is a welcome guest, but he or she is not invited to participate as a full member of the community. When a student meets a faculty member in a department office to ask a question about an exam, he or she is a welcome "visitor" to the academic unit but surely not a member of the departmental community.

Within academic affairs, managing relations among the program, the college administration, departments, and individual faculty is also a challenge for the living-learning community. Too often the living-learning program is considered marginal in terms of academic credibility or centrality to the research mission, and it requires departmental resources while only serving a subset of the student population. Recruiting tenured faculty is another major challenge for living-learning programs. Institutions often create disincentives for junior faculty to work in these kinds of scholarly, interdisciplinary, teaching-focused, and community-based programs.

The living-learning program's partnership and association with student affairs contributes to its perceived lack of credibility. Some faculty who are familiar with such programs but not participants in them may refer to them with disparagement as primarily "housing" with little to no academic credibility. Meanwhile, some student affairs and housing personnel may, like faculty, resent that living-learning programs skim precious budget dollars for a few entitled students while leaving less financial support for the majority of students. Staff may also argue that such programs create a constant flow of extra work and special exceptions to the traditional work flow. Such disparaging attitudes from academic and student affairs contribute greatly to institutionalized distrust and lack of support for living-learning programs.

Faculty and student affairs staff working in living-learning programs, the very boundary crossers seeking to work in the borderlands between academic and student affairs, often feel the brunt of such institutional divisions. Administrative support and resources may dwindle while disparagement and resentment become more prevalent. As a result, there is a higher frustration level among the faculty and staff in these scholarly communities than one might expect, thus leading to significant turnover and little opportunity for advancement in the field of residentially based academic programs. It is essential that faculty and staff working together in these programs value each other and enter the partnership as allies so as not to be distracted from that partnership by institutional divisions.

Snapshots of Successful Programs: University of Missouri at Columbia—Freshman Interest Group (FIG) Program (Frankie Minor, http://www.missouri.edu/~figwww)

This program began in 1995 and currently has over 1,200 first-year students participating in more than eighty FIG sections (general education courses). Seventy percent of the faculty mentors are tenured or tenure-track faculty. Funding has come from the chancellor and provost, but the largest percentages more recently have come from student affairs and residential life.

FIGs are intended to assist first-year students in making a successful transition from high school to college and provide them with a good foundation for academic and personal success. Small clusters of no more than twenty students are co-enrolled in three of the same classes and a one-credit seminar and live together in the same residence hall. Each FIG has an upper-division student peer adviser and a faculty mentor assigned to the group, and together they co-teach the seminar class. Students are given the opportunity for co-enrollment in courses for the second semester, and about 80 percent choose to do so. There is not a seminar requirement in the second semester.

Key Challenges

The program has become a signature element of the undergraduate program and institutional identity but still has not been fully incorporated in the fiscal planning structure for the university. Each year coordinators advertise, recruit, and assign students to this program without any firm commitment to its financial support as late as a month before it begins. The FIG Program has required new ways of thinking and modifications to existing services and programs. In some areas, the modifications and "out of the box" thinking have been easy; others continue to be a significant challenge. The institution is not used to this type of "hybrid" program, which does not fit either in academic or student affairs but someplace in between. The inability of established campus policies, procedures, and structures to account for this type of hybrid program may lead to confusion or indecision as to how to treat the program and its operational elements. Finally, as the success of the FIG Program has grown, pressure to expand the program has been significant.

Points of Sustainability

The ability of the two coordinators, the associate dean for Arts and Sciences and the director of Residential Life, to demonstrate true partnership and willingness to compromise has been essential in the success of the program. The success and popularity of the FIG Program with students, parents, and faculty has been very important. The gains in satisfaction, retention, and academic success have won public support from senior-level administrators, who have presented the program as evidence of successful programs to the state, resulting in the release of additional funds. The FIG Program has received support from a wide variety of academic programs and student affairs staff throughout the university. Academic divisions, departments, and colleges within the university have increasingly recognized the value of this program and more aggressively recommend this program to incoming students and identify faculty to participate in the program. It has also spawned related programs for transfer students (TRIGs) and new freshmen entering during the second semester.

Administrative and Budgetary Support

Another critical challenge for living-learning programs is securing a permanent institutional budget line. These programs often do not fit neatly in traditional funding categories such as academic departments or residence halls. As such, they may be supported through patchwork funding or reviewed only after other priorities are addressed. The patchwork model can work for a new program or when there is a supportive administrator, but it is not a long-term solution. As a result, these programs sometimes find themselves hailed on and off campus as being at the core of the undergraduate mission, yet in practice their funding prospects are tenuous from year to year or they are sorely underfunded. Living-learning program faculty and administrators need to persuade their supporting unit(s) to make the program budget a permanent line.

Faculty and staff involvement in living-learning programs is based on commitment to the ideals these programs represent. Administrative support for these programs, however, is often tied to more quantifiable measures such as student recruitment, retention, needs of particular student populations, and housing occupancy rates. Although these goals need not conflict with the broader visionary goals of living-learning programs, that tension often exists. Particularly in tighter budgetary times, administrators seek to realize instrumental gains at a lower cost. Conflicts can arise when there is pressure to achieve high retention rates, even if it means a less intensive community, fewer faculty resources, more traditional modes of teaching, and fewer staff. Similarly, the success of a program can lead to unexpected challenges. If a program is so successful with x number of students, then why not expand the program to all students on campus? Challenges arise when the mandate to expand comes without a comparable budget increment and without regard to issues of deep community and learning.

Snapshots of Successful Programs: University of Illinois/ Urbana-Champaign—Unit One (Howard Schein, http://www.housing.uiuc.edu/living/unit1)

Unit One first started in 1971. It now has 650 students, about thirty instructors, and over a thousand enrolled students each semester. Unit One hosts six to eight guests-in-residence per academic year, who serve one- to two-week residencies. The budget is shared by the housing division and the provost, with a significant portion from student funds. "The mission for Unit One is to create a small, liberal arts environment within the university that is intense and intellectually stimulating, and one that combines students' academic and personal concerns in credit and non-credit activities and programs." With the new surge of constructing residential learning communities, Unit One remains the "flagship" program.

Key Challenges

The only challenge to Unit One's existence came more than twenty years ago. The College of Liberal Arts and Sciences eliminated Unit One, primarily for budgetary reasons, ostensibly due to the college's claim that Unit One was not academically credible. Students (and their parents) successfully lobbied the campus to reconsider Unit One's demise. The vice-chancellor for student affairs and the provost restructured the program, enacted a significant student fee, and housed the academic sponsorship in the provost's office with strong faculty oversight. Since that time, Unit One has thrived without challenges to its existence and without financial problems.

Points of Sustainability

Unit One is an integral part of the housing division within student affairs and receives very strong support. The provost has been consistently supportive in providing the necessary funds for the academic component of the program. Unit One has brought good publicity to the university's undergraduate education mission. Student and parent enthusiasm has always been a strong contributing factor. Faculty note student performance in terms of intellectuality and interactivity. Students "advertise" the program to other faculty and to their high schools. Their responses in all evaluations put the program in a very positive light. Unit One is very flexible and "opportunistic." For example, Unit One's array of courses can change each semester, and invited guests can be geared to students' requests. In the "old days," Unit One was seen to be on the fringe, but in the past twenty years, it has become academically credible and has developed good ties to many academic units and student affairs units. For most faculty members, however, programs like Unit One only become of interest when they participate or when their children participate.

Faculty Involvement

In many respects, the characteristics of living-learning programs resonate with the reasons that most faculty have chosen to enter academia. They relish the image of the scholarly community in which learning, scholarship, community, and faculty and students all come together as one. At the same time, the demands of most universities inhibit faculty from becoming involved in the programs. Faculty's lives and rewards are centered in disciplinary work, departmental structures for teaching and service, and research and publishing. Deep involvement with students, interdisciplinary teaching and scholarship, and work away from the department all challenge the typical faculty role that has been institutionalized and rewarded on so many campuses.

As a result, it can be difficult for some living-learning programs to recruit faculty. It is worthwhile, however, to examine which faculty members join and why they make a commitment to these programs. Typically, faculty who participate in these programs are independent-minded, have moved away from a career that depends on the traditional reward structure, are tenured or not on a tenure-track, and have decided to pursue the dream of the scholarly community regardless of institutional norms and rewards. Many faculty are not fully satisfied with the academic lives they have found in their departments or on their campuses. They want something more engaging. Once these faculty join a living-learning program, they embrace their newfound interdisciplinary, faculty colleagues and the engaged students in the living-learning program. They cite the diversity of people and ideas, the thematic focus of the program, and the opportunity and encouragement to innovate in their teaching and take intellectual risks with their students and colleagues as additional benefits. Monetary or other material rewards can and do make a difference, but in the long term, the quality of the experience is the enduring factor for sustained faculty involvement.

Snapshots of Successful Programs: St. Lawrence University, The First-Year Program (FYP) (Steven Horwitz, http://web.stlawu.edu/fyp)

The program became mandatory for all first-year students in the fall of 1988. Currently, there are about 570 students involved in seventeen team-taught courses in the fall and thirty-six individually taught seminars in the spring. Students are divided into groups of thirty-two, with two faculty assigned to them as instructors-advisers. These groups also live together. The central mission of the FYP is holistic, integrated liberal inquiry with the ultimate goal of creating a campus culture that is more serious in purpose and more academically engaged. Over the years, the program has become very much mainstreamed on campus. The vast majority of our financial support comes from academic affairs.

Key Challenges

We've had a compensation package that enables faculty whose FYP teaching includes a slight overload to get that back in the form of a semester's leave after a three-year commitment. Still, when resources are tight, making the case for this generous policy can be a challenge. The perception of political correctness and a soft curriculum, as well as doubts about the viability of teaching out of one's discipline, dogged the program for many years. This seems to have quieted with the program's gradual institutionalization and the new faculty who have entered the program. The FYP falls under academic affairs, but with its residential foundation, the program works closely with Student Life to ensure meaningful integration. The relationship has gone back and forth over the years; finding the right balance and grounds for a cooperative, productive relationship remains an ongoing challenge.

Points of Sustainability

The driving force is that the program was created by faculty. Faculty were concerned about a lack of intellectual purpose and a social, residential life that undermined attempts at serious academic work. Had the program been implemented from "on high," it may not have survived the twists and turns of the intervening years. Having had so many FYP faculty (78 of 165 faculty on campus have taught in the program) has been crucial to our success over time. Another key element has been administrative support. That support has come at crucial times and has enabled us to grow, evolve, and become institutionalized. The program also works for students and is very attractive to parents of prospective students. Faculty are exposed to new pedagogies and receive constructive feedback from colleagues in a team-teaching environment, and they take the skills they develop back to their departments and programs. This makes it easier to support and sustain the program.

Sustained Leadership

The most successful programs typically have directors who remain with their programs for a significant amount of time. Due to the fragility of cross-campus partnerships and the marginality of living-learning programs, institutional success for such programs is often linked to director longevity. Directors who gain the confidence of academic or student affairs administrators are less likely to become frustrated by the challenges of boundary crossing and budgetary instability and thus are better able to sustain and lead their programs.

Running a living-learning program is like leading a small college. The director is required to both represent the program in institutional matters and to have hands-on involvement with faculty, students, curriculum, and assessment. The work can be stressful and time-consuming, especially with limited support staff. In the informal national network of living-learning faculty and staff, only a very small number of individuals have built and sustained professional careers solely associated with living-learning programs.

Diversity

That living-learning programs present opportunities for developing diverse scholarly communities that model the changing racial and ethnic demographics of society and contribute to the intellectual and social development of students as part of a democratic education is obvious (Schoem, 2001; Schoem and Pasque, 2003). It is disappointing, therefore, that so few programs reflect such diversity. Many programs appear satisfied to maintain a cohort of students from homogeneous racial and social class backgrounds. Other programs choose a theme that appeals to a single demographic group or narrowly targets an ethnic group to a program so a broader heterogeneous population typically does not enroll. Successful programs maintain diversity through intentional recruitment, outreach, and sustained attention to the academic support and intergroup relations of community members. (Diversity in learning communities is discussed in Chapter Seven).

Student Engagement and Community Building

Although these programs are built upon the notion of a close and involved community, some living-learning programs still suffer from a disengaged student body. One might assume that the involvement of student affairs would ensure an active and lively student community, but that is not always the case. In some cases, the challenge is that a living-learning program is not sufficiently balanced between academics and social integration. There may be strong curriculum and faculty but not enough attention to community. In other cases, there is so much concern for managing civil behavior in the residence hall that the environment does not allow for student experimentation and creativity. Another challenge is that limited staffing puts a strain on the kind of staff mentoring needed to encourage community building.

Living-learning programs must trust students and empower them to take leadership roles in terms of community building, social responsibility, programming, and budget. Without student participation—even control—of program activities, it is not enough for faculty and program directors to invite outstanding speakers and then expect interest or a respectable student turnout. The work of building student leadership programs and guiding student leaders requires considerable energy and planning on the part of program directors and faculty.

Assessment

The assessment challenges within living-learning programs are similar to those faced by nonresidential programs. (Chapter Six discusses assessment in greater detail.) Living-learning program administrators and faculty may be interested in assessment, but they lack evaluation training, there are limited funds for assessment, there is restricted access to data, or the type of information requested by the administration is different from what is of interest to faculty. Campus leadership may be interested in outcomes closely related to institutional measures of success such as recruitment, retention, or graduation data. A common interest, however, may be outcomes related to student achievement. When administration and program leadership agree on common goals and uses for data, then assessment may lead to increased visibility for the program, more resources, and program improvements. In an era of accountability, however, campus administration may ask for particular data, so it is important to regularly plan for assessment and annually collect information such as who participates in the program and how they are doing.

Snapshots of Successful Programs: University of Southern Maine, Russell Scholars Program (Stephen Romanoff, http://www.usm.maine.edu/~rscholar)

The Russell Scholars Program (RSP) began in 1996 and has an enrollment of approximately two hundred students, one faculty-director, five part-time faculty, and one half-time secretary. RSP offers approximately ten general education courses, some in rotation, concentrating on the first two years, but also offering a few advanced courses for upperclassmen such as Senior Capstone. RSP reports directly to the provost.

After seven successful years and national recognition, the program remains marginal because of its relative newness. The word *scholars* may imply an honors program and exclusivity, neither of which is the case with RSP. However, the name seems to motivate students who participate in RSP, adding some prestige and dignity to the extra rigor in the program. The key focus of RSP is community building through mentoring and collaboration, both within the program and beyond. The RSP philosophy is: Within an interdisciplinary, residential learning community, students will attain their educational goals through mentoring, collaborative learning, collaborative teaching, service learning, and out-of-class activities.

Key Challenges

The key challenges have been (1) the absence of any additional full- or half-time appointments to the faculty, (2) a budget to support faculty appointments and to offer a broader curriculum, and (3) institutionalized support from the general faculty.

Points of Sustainability

RSP has achieved a seven-year retention average of over 90 percent and a 30 percent out-of-state recruitment rate, along with high credits earned and graduation rates. Subsequently, RSP is now funded from the university's capital fund and appears to have earned its place at USM as a viable recruiting and retention vehicle and as a pathway by which students may receive general education instruction. Although student housing and student affairs have not directly supported RSP financially, RSP is coordinating with them for the purposes of modifying housing and student activities. While the RSP director's full-time administration of and teaching within the program are also key to its continuity, a small dedicated core of part-time and overload-teaching, tenured faculty have remained with the program, allowing RSP to thrive.

Risk Taking and Innovation

Risk taking and innovation in both the intellectual and social spheres of college life are two of the hallmarks of living-learning programs. An early report on the success of the Pilot Program and Residential College at the University of Michigan (Hatch, 1972) comments on this very issue: "The Pilot Program, however 'successful' by traditional standards, does encompass programs that border on the heretical, that are unpredictable, capable of failure, or less controlling of students. Many aspects of such innovations cannot be evaluated fairly or adequately to the satisfaction of either their advocates or their opponents. The Pilot Program nonetheless represents a type of experimentation that requires courage and genuine involvement and responsibility on the part of administrators, faculty, graduate staff, and students; it demands freedom to succeed and *to fail*" (p. 9).

Unfortunately, there are significant structural barriers to creating strong programs. Often what makes a program memorable in any given year is the very course, program, or student leadership activity that is unique to that particular living-learning community. At the same time, marginal programs have little room for mistakes. College administrators, faculty, student affairs staff, and even students themselves can place a disproportionate amount of attention on a risk gone wrong in a living-learning program. These programs require an innovative edge and involve faculty, students, and staff willing to take educational risks.

Characteristics of Successful Programs

The good news about the challenges facing living-learning programs is that many programs face obstacles, overcome them, and continue to succeed over time. Several successful programs have been highlighted throughout this chapter as models of sustainability. A review of established living-learning programs suggests some common elements for program improvement and sustainability: director commitment, faculty involvement, strong relationships between academic and student affairs, administrative champions, program quality, and student leadership.

Director Commitment

Much of the success of any particular living-learning program is due to the commitment and effort of the director. Directors are committed to the ideals of the program and the intrinsic rewards that result. Regrettably, the typical package does not include high salary, status, or a light workload. Rewards, however, might include recognition of faculty leadership in living-learning programs as a contribution toward teaching and service in tenure considerations, inclusion in meetings of departmental chairs and directors, funds for travel to national conferences, encouragement and support for research and publications, and opportunities to be involved as a core member in other aspects of university life and leadership. Public recognition goes a long way in rewarding the committed faculty and staff of living-learning communities. Programs thrive when senior administrators who are responsible for oversight of living-learning programs find ways to support directors, faculty, and students.

Faculty Involvement

Faculty participation in the creation, maintenance, and improvement of the program is crucial. Faculty champions help raise program quality and provide political support to help overcome the various challenges programs often face. Faculty also play a valuable role in promoting the living-learning program across the campus. With faculty support, it is possible for living-learning programs to move from the margins to the core of institutional life.

Management of Academic Affairs and Student Affairs Relations

Successful programs find ways to overcome institutional structures and barriers that actively work against the philosophical and practical collaboration and partnership that are a core of these programs' identity. When academic and student affairs staff look beyond the institutional barriers that often divide them, they see their common commitments to undergraduate education and learning. Providing support and independent space for the faculty and student affairs staff in the living-learning program who work daily to build a partnership between the two units will go a long way toward building effective and mutually rewarding partnerships.

Administrative Champions

Successful living-learning programs typically have the support of one or more influential administrators such as a student affairs vice president, the provost, the president, a college dean, or another senior leader. This support may be demonstrated through permanent financial support for the program. Administrative support typically follows when and if the goals and outcomes for the living-learning program are connected to the institutional mission and goals (e.g., student recruitment and retention, commitment to undergraduate education, filling housing spaces, parental involvement, alumni support).

Program Quality

Living-learning programs are held to high standards. Word of mouth, campus media, and national networks contribute to how faculty members view the academic credibility of a program as well as how students and parents perceive program value. Assessment results also contribute to the local and national reputation of the program.

The Michigan Community Scholars Program is well known for its cross-disciplinary faculty, who are known on campus as outstanding teachers. The program is also recognized for its emphasis on diversity, intercultural engagement, student leadership, and community partnerships. Bowling Green State University's Chapman College is recognized for its successful student retention and dedicated faculty. Iowa State University is known for its assessment work on learning communities and for its model collaboration between academic affairs and student affairs. Yale's Residential Colleges are noted for both their history and tradition, as well as their continued centrality to the life of the university.

Snapshots of Successful Programs: Bowling Green State University (BGSU), Chapman Learning Community (Thomas Klein, http://www.bgsu.edu/colleges/clc)

Chapman began in 1997 and averages 170 students annually. There are sixteen faculty teaching in the program and about fifteen to twenty-five courses a semester. First-year Chapman students enroll in at least one core, general education course each semester held in our newly renovated Kohl Hall, with its two million dollar state-of-the-art learning community; in addition, they take a one-hour field experiences course each semester that covers community events tied to academic themes. Chapman also provides special programming, including study sessions, leadership training programs, social activities, group dinners, outdoor adventures, and increased involvement with community service and student organizations on campus. Chapman promotes civic and moral engagement. Chapman started out in the provost's office and in 1999 was moved to the College of Arts and Sciences. The Office of Residence Life has led the way in prodding the campus culture to support the living-learning community revolution. To the degree that Chapman has been heralded by the local press and the university marketing staff, it is not marginal. The inclusion of BGSU's LCs in the recent *U.S. News & World Report* has given us increased visibility from key community and educational leaders. And since there are now twelve other living-learning communities on campus and the success rates of our students have been high (as measured by our office of institutional research), Chapman is widely perceived as effective. Some faculty resent the living-learning experiment on this campus; many do not understand it, and many, in financially challenging times, see the program as robbing departments of needed resources. Still, the great majority of faculty have been either supportive or quiet about our successes.

Key Challenges

The permanence or impermanence of our faculty positions has been a troubling issue. There is now a very good working relationship with admissions and residence life, ensuring that recruitment of students will happen steadily and persistently. As the university adds more living-learning communities, it's easier to recruit students. Our greatest current challenge has been competing for students with a new themed community that is the president's darling. BGX (Bowling Green Experience) will soon offer a welcome-days experience and a general education course in the critical examination of values to all BGSU students. Ironically, as Chapman will include these sections for all its students, we and other LCs might benefit from this new development.

The home college has increased the faculty teaching load (to 3/2 in a semester plan) and has taken away some release time. However, in exchange, the faculty have been promised continuing lectureships beyond the present five-year term appointments and will be able to teach one of their five courses in their department.

Points of Sustainability

Support from administration and the program's success have been the two most important sustaining factors. The president, provost, and arts and sciences dean understand the philosophy of the living-learning symbiosis and have been willing to support it significantly.

Our success has been defined by positive retention, grade and satisfaction results, and positive student reactions to the program. A study by the BGSU Office of

Institutional Research has confirmed this success. Many Chapman students have gone on to take leadership positions on campus, spreading the word that Chapman is an excellent program.

Student Empowerment and Leadership

Students are important to the campuswide perception of the program. Students from living-learning programs frequently take on leadership roles throughout the campus. Students can also return to living-learning programs as resident advisers, peer advisers, co-teachers in seminars, or as tutors. As program graduates receive academic recognition, they contribute greatly to the program's reputation among administrators, faculty, and student affairs staff.

Conclusion

Each living-learning program is unique and exists within its own university and college context. A broad liberal arts emphasis is practical for some programs and campuses, whereas a thematic focus may be more appropriate for others. For some programs, a high degree of budgetary control is often cited as an important factor in program sustainability, while others succeed because they have dedicated faculty lines. What living-learning programs share, however, is interdependence with the wider college or university community.

Living-learning programs continue to flourish on college campuses because they are characterized by learning and community in higher education. In their ideal form, they represent a scholarly community, emphasize deep learning for an engaged and diverse community, integrate the academic and social experiences of college life, and exemplify the most innovative and liberating practices of democratic education.

CHAPTER NINE

NEXT STEPS

Expanding Our Understanding of Communities of Learning

Throughout this volume and in our earlier book, *Creating Learning Communities,* we focus primarily on different aspects of campus-based learning communities. Although this book presents deeper discussions of the issues that contribute to sustaining and improving learning communities (campus cultures, curriculum, pedagogy, faculty development, diversity, living-learning communities, and assessment), certainly much remains to be studied, researched, and reported about college learning communities. It is also important to recognize that higher education did not invent the concept of learning communities, nor do all college-based learning communities limit their activities to their campuses. In this concluding chapter, we expand the lens on learning communities and link learning communities to current movements and issues in higher education and society at large. This chapter addresses three related, but distinctly different, trends: college learning communities that are designed to build bridges connecting the campus to the community, learning communities within the K–16 movement that are designed to bridge the gaps between K–12 schools and colleges and universities, and the recent trend toward "smaller learning communities" within the K–12 sector designed to enhance student achievement and teacher retention.

Learning Communities That Foster Civic Engagement

Over the past several years, universities and colleges have been charged repeatedly to actively embrace their responsibility to promote civic values and to
strengthen our democratic society. In the post 9/11 world, there is an ever greater
expectation that colleges and universities will structure education to meet the demand for an active, democratic citizenry.

In 1998, the National Commission on Civic Renewal issued a report addressing the civic health of the nation. The commission, created and supported
by the Pew Charitable Trusts, was cochaired by William Bennett and Sam Nunn
and directed by William Galston, former domestic policy adviser to President
Clinton. The commission measured civic health along several dimensions—participation in electoral politics, political and social trust, voluntary sector activity,
and attitudes and conduct bearing on the moral condition of society, to name but
a few. Commission researchers concluded that although not all these trends move
in the same direction, political participation and all forms of trust have declined
significantly in the past generation. Their work has spawned additional national
reports and recommendations that, when broadly interpreted, have implications
for the learning communities movement.

In 2002, the American Association of State Colleges and Universities
(AASCU) published a major report, "Stepping Forward as Stewards of Place"
(2002), which charged college presidents and chancellors to translate the rhetoric
of engagement into reality. The report acknowledged the multiple ways that colleges and universities link their communities with the world at large, challenging
them to take a leadership role in addressing the multitude of issues facing our communities and our regions. AASCU defined "public engagement" as place related,
interactive, mutually beneficial, and integrated (p. 7). When read closely, this definition of "public engagement" mirrors the language we use to describe campuswide learning communities. Many higher education institutions have found that
learning communities foster public engagement by placing high value on involving students in different forms of service learning and community service.

Following closely on the heels of the AASCU report, in 2003 the Association of American Colleges and Universities (AACU) and Campus Compact established a new Institute for Liberal Learning and Civic Engagement to make
civic engagement in a diverse and interconnected world more central to faculty
work and student learning in higher education. According to Troy Duster, chair
of the AACU board, "Several recent AACU initiatives have called for higher
education to focus national attention on the goals of college learning in the
twenty-first century. AACU has consistently argued that we must expand our

vision of college learning beyond just a vocational or professional focus to encompass students' civic and ethical responsibilities in a diverse democracy and fractured global community." Again, learning communities arise in these recommendations as a vehicle for engaging students and faculty in civic responsibility (Association of American Colleges and Universities, 2003).

Simultaneously with AACU's report, the Carnegie Foundation for the Advancement of Teaching published a report on moral and civic education at more than one hundred colleges. After a three-year study, the authors concluded that higher education is not doing a good job of integrating civic education into the undergraduate experience. In the report, *Educating Citizens: Preparing America's Undergraduates for Lives of Moral and Civic Responsibility* (Colby, Ehrlich, Beaumont, and Stephens, 2003), the authors cite examples of how institutions incorporate civic education into their curricula through volunteer community service programs. However, they conclude that these volunteer programs are not reaching the students who need them most. The authors suggest that civic engagement is best taught by recognizing that the learning experiences most likely to produce real results will take place (1) through intentional co-curricular activities planned collaboratively between academic units and residence halls and cafeterias, (2) through extracurricular programs, and (3) by revising curriculum to integrate civic problems as a theme in a variety of interdisciplinary programs, such as learning communities.

Intentional Civic Engagement in a Learning Community

In response to the growing awareness and interest in reaffirming the civic education mission of public higher education, a number of colleges and universities have instituted civics-related programs. A relatively new program at the University of Maryland, CIVICUS, is organized around this intentional outcome of higher education—encouraging greater civic engagement. CIVICUS, housed in the College of Behavioral and Social Sciences, is based upon the concepts of leadership, citizenship, scholarship, community service, and the development of a diverse community (http://www.bsos.umd.edu/handbook_civicus.html).

This is an interesting co-joining of themes. CIVICUS supports student self-governance through a close-knit society. CIVICUS is not built around an interdisciplinary academic theme (like science, technology and society, or international studies), nor is it designed around career interests (like preengineers) or learning styles (like developmental models). Rather, the primary raison d'être for this community is to involve students and faculty in a very overt way in building a civil society.

The students in the program are given the status of "associates" and are given a unique opportunity to build a "civil society" in their residence hall. The process of creating this residential community involves all associates, who share common readings, special programs, guest speakers, and experiential learning, including community service. All CIVICUS students are expected to demonstrate their commitment to the program through

- Membership and involvement in a CIVICUS standing committee
- Participation in planned CIVICUS community service activities
- Active contribution to the development, implementation, and evaluation of the hall governance and community living guidelines

First-year associates take a common core of courses dealing with the interdisciplinary issues of civil society. There is an emphasis on residence hall governance and leadership development. All CIVICUS associates are also encouraged to attend campus lectures on preserving and building a civil society.

The Role of Service Learning in Fostering Civic Engagement

As we have noted earlier, learning communities function to change both the institution and the student's experience of higher education, often through a required or integrated service learning component. Thomas Ehrlich (2000) described the "value added" nature of higher education in these terms: "Unless [universities] can not only promise but also deliver something more than job training, their role in society will decline. That 'something more' must include, as Dewey taught us, a focused concern on the civic responsibility of colleges and universities, to and within their communities, and on the civic capacities of the student whom they are educating" (p. iii).

A concrete outcome of Ehrlich's work has been the validation of, and subsequent significant increase in, service learning opportunities on our campuses. The National Center for Educational Statistics defines service learning as "curriculum-based community service that integrates classroom instruction with community service activities" (Skinner and Chapman, 1999, p. 3). Over the past decade, we have experienced rapid growth in this curricular innovation across the K–16 spectrum. As of last year, 32 percent of all public schools had incorporated service learning into their curricula, including a remarkable 46 percent of high schools. Well over half of the colleges and universities in the United States have signed on with the Campus Compact, a consortium of colleges committed to service learning.

One measure of this increasing interest in service learning can be seen in the number and variety of learning communities that actively promote service learning. In a recent survey of learning communities posted on the National Learning Communities Project website, over 70 percent of the programs listed service learning as a key component of their programs (http://learningcommons.evergreen.edu). When faculty and students are asked why they value service learning experiences, they emphasize the sense of community that service learning fosters in the personal growth of students. Dahl (1995) explained in his essay, "Participation and the Problem of Civic Understanding," in *Rights and the Common Good,* that good citizens exhibit the qualities of moral reasoning and open-mindedness; they are informed and empathetic. Although we may see the qualities of good citizenship as the mark of a well-educated person, the benefits of service learning go beyond individual growth to the mission of higher education in the community at large. Service learning contributes to the institution's role in the city or town and the state as well. Service learning components of learning communities help to bridge the "town-gown" dichotomy that sometimes exists around large universities.

Learning communities incorporate service learning in many different ways. Community service components of learning communities vary from programs structured specifically around service learning to programs where service learning is merely one small assignment in one course that is part of a much larger community curriculum.

Portland State University Portland State redesigned its curriculum in a way that allowed it to bring learning communities into the public schools and aimed to have an impact on the community at large. The Senior Inquiry Project is a senior-year high school course based on the university's Freshman Inquiry course. The course is taught by teams of high school teachers and university faculty partnered with peer or undergraduate mentors from the university. Students who complete the program successfully and attend PSU earn fifteen credits and move into required sophomore-level course work in general education.

The Portland State Freshman Inquiry course is described as a unique type of learning community. It achieves the status of "learning community" through a combination of team teaching and interdisciplinary themes (http://www.ous.pdx.edu/frinq/index.html). The program creates a unique interdisciplinary environment that crosses boundaries between university and the school and forges strong bonds between students and faculty. It also provides real-time, professional development experiences for school teachers and university faculty that change how both partners do their work.

University of Maryland College Park College Park Scholars at the University of
Maryland has an extensive, fully integrated service learning program that includes service learning in the seminar courses as well as in the capstone experience of the program. Projects have included creating a directory of local
child-care facilities for students, faculty, and staff of the university; long-term
tutoring programs in the elementary schools (in conjunction with America Reads
and America Counts programs); developing and designing hands-on science
after-school programs for local schools; and many other projects. The mayor
of College Park regularly addresses the students, and it is not uncommon for students to develop long-term relationships with their service sites.

Learning communities are well positioned to take the lead in this arena, in
part because learning communities depend on participatory involvement from
all the diverse members of "their community," more so than traditional curricular structures (such as majors or departments). Learning communities neatly
weave together academic, residential, student affairs, and co-curricular components toward a common goal.

Although overall the evaluation of specific service learning programs yields
mixed results, a massive study of more than twenty-two thousand college students by Alexander Astin and his colleagues (2000) has found that the positive
effects of service by individual students are amplified by discussion of service experiences among students. Service learning is especially effective in generating
positive attitudes and behaviors toward civic engagement because it is structured
to encourage such student-to-student discussion.

Service learning has proven to be a robust component of learning communities. Service learning alone, however, will not accomplish the broader goal of
increasing civic engagement of college students. Yet learning communities are
especially well positioned to promote the intentional goal and broader mission
of higher education: preparing students to assume their full civic responsibilities
in a democratic society.

Expanding Communities by Linking Schools and Colleges Through K–16 Partnerships

K–16 (or P–16) is a shorthand way of viewing all of public education as a seamless continuum stretching from preschool to the baccalaureate degree. This
perspective encourages new ways of thinking about complex issues such as educational standards and accountability, the alignment of college admissions policies and secondary education graduation standards, school governance, finance,
and teacher preparation. K–16 work poses a challenge to traditional higher

education assumptions. The culture of higher education has a low tolerance for work in the K–12 community outside colleges of education. The current reward structure is not designed to value faculty investment and involvement with the public schools or public school teachers. Yet there are persistent and increasingly strong voices calling for such engagement that have potential to dramatically change the current dynamics.

In 1999, the American Council on Education Presidents' Task Force on Teacher Education released *To Touch the Future: Transforming the Way Teachers Are Taught*. This report laid the groundwork for college and university leaders to actively and aggressively reform the way their institutions educate future teachers. Specifically, presidents were called upon to "move the education of teachers to the center of their professional and institutional agendas" (p. 3). The past two U.S. presidents (Clinton and Bush) have made the K–12 reform agenda among their highest priorities and have directed millions of dollars of grants to promote school-university partnerships. The landmark education legislation, No Child Left Behind (2002 NCLB) and the Higher Education Reauthorization Act (2003–2004), leave no ambiguity about the federal intention to influence higher education to engage more directly with public schools to address teacher quality, student learning, access to college, and standards.

No individual institution or K–12 community can carry the flag alone on any of these issues. Rather, K–16 partnerships recognize the need for universities to collaborate with public schools to operationally define college readiness and support public schools to ensure that all high school graduates are college-ready by redesigning teacher preparation as a joint effort.

It is not surprising that higher education and the public schools have discovered their interdependence—what is surprising is that it took so long. Learning communities are an obvious vehicle for these K–16 partnerships. There is no question that colleges and universities share common ground with public schools. Across the country, university systems, community college systems, and public school systems are collaborating and exploring innovative relationships. As challenging as it is to construct interdisciplinary learning communities that transcend traditional academic departments and university administrative divisions, it is that much more difficult to cross between education segments: between high schools and community colleges and between two-year and four-year institutions. A number of states have begun to engage in K–16 activities that bring together faculty and teachers across the continuum from public schools through college in order to improve teaching and learning, raise student achievement, and prepare all students for college. Several of these pioneer K–16 initiatives have used learning communities as a model for bringing faculty and teachers together to solve shared problems.

Bowling Green State University: Partners in Context and Community

One of the residential learning communities at Bowling Green State University (BGSU), Partners in Context and Community (PCC), is designed for students planning to teach in high-poverty urban schools (http://www.bgsu.edu/colleges/as/pcc/developPro.html). Supported by a five-year grant from the U.S. Department of Education Teacher Quality Enhancement Program (TQE), the project builds a residential learning community experience to support and encourage students who are interested in teaching in urban school districts. According to project director Bob Midden (personal communication, February 2003), in their first year, students in PCC live in the same residence hall in which the PCC staff and core faculty offices are located. Two of their courses (English composition and Introduction to Education) are fully integrated with field experiences in which students work in urban schools for about four hours each week. These courses are team-taught, with classes combined as a block and linked by the theme of urban education. The theme is realized through assignments in the linked classes: in English composition, writing assignments are devoted to issues of urban education; in the Introduction to Education course, assignments are linked to the actual experiences of the students in the schools. Field experiences offer a rich source of writing and reflection in both courses. Faculty in the program supervise the field experiences.

The learning community also sponsors co-curricular activities that extend learning beyond the formal classroom environment. For example, one class visited a large and very popular hands-on science museum in Toledo, where students explored the exhibits and learned ways they could use that type of resource to enrich learning for the students they will someday teach. On another occasion, the program sponsored an interactive storyteller. Of all their activities, students report they value field experiences the most (http://www.bgsu.edu/colleges/as/pcc/).

University System of Maryland "Learning in Communities" Project (LINC)

Project LINC is another creative approach to building bridges between universities and schools. Like the Bowling Green project, LINC is supported by one of the first U.S. Department of Education Title II Teacher Quality Enhancement Grants. The University System of Maryland brought three universities (University of Maryland, Towson University, and Bowie State University) into partnerships with three public schools to create professional development schools (PDS), which were established as learning communities. University faculty and school district teachers and administrators collectively plan and deliver professional development programs for preservice teachers, novice, and uncertified teachers in challenging schools. By bringing courses and projects off campus to the school site, this innovative project builds bridges and is more acutely responsive to the public school needs.

All the lessons learned from the learning communities movement are brought to bear on these K–16 initiatives–from the collaborative planning committees to creative budgets and scheduling to co-curricular and service opportunities–to establish permanent school-university partnerships that are greater than the sum of their parts.

Hampshire College

Hampshire College offers yet another example of higher education reaching out to public schools to create communities of educators (college teachers and school teachers). In the current public education climate, with standardized state and national tests haunting teachers in underperforming schools, universities must be willing to step up to the plate to join with their colleagues in the K–12 schools to develop and model instructional practices designed to increase student motivation, engagement, and success. Madelaine Marquez, project director and director of the Center for Innovative Education at Hampshire College, directs a project that has built a learning community of teachers around collaborative work, self-reflection, and peer coaching. During the three-week summer program, teachers support each other as they explore Hampshire's model of using student-led investigations to teach academically challenging yet appealing curricula about essential ideas and principles in the sciences (http://cie.hampshire.edu).

Participating college faculty and teachers spend a week in class reviewing content knowledge and pedagogical strategies that are practiced with student "campers" in a two-week science camp. The scientific investigations and engineering challenges presented to the students in the summer program highlight the value of guided exploration to deepen student understanding of content, encourage classroom discourse about ideas, and promote a sense of team accomplishment. Teachers reflect daily about their teaching, conduct classroom videotaping, and offer peer feedback. Throughout the school year the class videotaping and peer support continues. Thus, the college teachers and the high school teachers form their own "learning community" or "community of practice" to explore and expand their understanding of their disciplines and the teaching of science.

Lessons to Be Learned from Public School Reform

Learning communities in higher education share roots with reform efforts in K–12 schools. Historical studies of the learning communities movement in higher education frequently cite John Dewey and Alexander Meiklejohn as early proponents of progressive, pragmatic, integrated, nontraditional educational pedagogies and curricular innovations in the K–12 segment. Over the past several decades, and with support from federal funds from the U.S. Department of Education, significant progress has been made in developing learning communities in the K–12 education arena. To better understand learning communities in context, it is helpful to take a closer look at the research and best practice described in K–12 literature.

In 1983, the U.S. Department of Education's National Commission on Excellence in Education published the report, *A Nation at Risk,* a document often cited as the beginning of current school reform efforts. The dramatic conclusion of this report raised the awareness of the American public to an emerging crisis in our public education system: "If an unfriendly power had attempted to impose on America the mediocre educational performance that exists today, we might well have viewed it as an act of war. As it stands, we have allowed this to happen to ourselves. We have even squandered the gains in achievement made in the wake of the Sputnik challenge. Moreover, we have dismantled essential support systems which helped make those gains possible. We have, in effect, been committing an act of unthinking, unilateral educational disarmament" (p. 5). The report raised an alarm that resonated around the country as different states and the federal government sought to identify and address the critical shortfall areas in public education. The commission advanced the following recommendations:

- Graduation requirements should be strengthened so that all students establish a foundation in five *new* basics: English, mathematics, science, social studies, and computer science.
- Schools and colleges should adopt higher and measurable standards for academic performance.
- The amount of time students spend engaged in learning should be significantly increased.
- The teaching profession should be strengthened through higher standards for preparation and professional growth.

A year later, in 1984, the National Institute of Education (NIE) issued a parallel report on undergraduate education titled *Involvement in Learning.* That report warned that higher education was failing to fulfill its potential and was ignoring important information on student achievement and retention. With more high school students attending college, and a society becoming increasingly dependent on a highly educated, technologically proficient workforce, the gaps between expectations and realities in undergraduate education were cause for concern.

The virtually simultaneous publication of these two studies suggests that even twenty years ago, one could begin to see a convergence of issues affecting both K–12 and higher education. When underprepared students graduated from high school, they failed to succeed in college and everyone suffered. When teachers graduated from college ill-prepared to teach to a challenging and diverse public school environment, everyone suffered.

Ever since *A Nation at Risk* was published in 1983, the American public has been on notice that our public schools are not responding appropriately to the challenge of educating all students to high standards. As we continue to examine the growing achievement gap across the country, we find that this gap is especially evident in urban areas, where large numbers of poor and minority students are falling farther behind.

Coalition of Essential Schools

Over the past twenty years, the K–12 community has responded in several ways to this challenge, and it is instructive for leaders in higher education to be informed of the K–12 reform efforts since colleges and universities educate their graduates. One of the first and most respected systemic responses was a movement founded by Ted Sizer of Brown University in 1984, the Coalition of Essential Schools (CES). Sizer's (1984) model is described in his book *Horace's Compromise.* That year, twelve high schools in seven states joined the Coalition, which is designed around a learning community model. Today, the Coalition of Essential Schools is a national network of schools and centers engaged in restructuring schools into smaller learning communities.

The Coalition schools share a set of ideas known as the Common Principles, which guide their reform efforts. The CES movement is one of the "whole school" reform movements–that is, reform conceived at the macro level rather than the individual teacher or classroom level. The CES requires that multiple stakeholders collaborate to arrive at shared goals and develop whole-school strategies and priorities. In a five-year study of American high schools, Sizer concluded that schools are often organized in ways that do not support student learning, such as fifty-minute periods, lecture, and drill. As a result, according to Sizer, students have little opportunity to think deeply about important issues or produce work that means anything to them. In response to these findings, Sizer formulated a set of principles designed to lead to better teaching and more genuine learning in American high schools. Central to his school reform movement was a commitment to the following principles: a commitment to personalized learning, a strong sense of community, mastery of a few essential subjects and skills (depth rather than breadth), and graduation by exhibition (performance assessments) rather than examination. Sizer's coalition has evolved and matured, and participating schools serve as models of engaged teaching and learning grounded in learning communities.

U.S. Department of Education Small Learning Communities

In the United States today, approximately 70 percent of American high school students attend schools enrolling more than a thousand students, and nearly half of all high school students attend schools enrolling more than 1,500 students. According to Williams (1990), an effective size for secondary school is in the range of four hundred to eight hundred students. Enrollment size has a strong effect on learning in schools with large concentrations of poor and minority children (Cotton, 1996).

Because the U.S. Department of Education intended to make significant investments in school reform, they turned to a broad range of research studies that confirmed that smaller learning environments contribute to boosting student achievement (Williams, 1990). According to studies by Raywid (1996) and Klonsky (1995), school size has positive effects on student outcomes (attendance rates, frequency of disciplinary actions, school loyalty).

Research ultimately confirms what parents intuitively believe–that smaller schools are safer and more productive because students feel less alienated, more nurtured, and more connected to caring adults, and teachers feel they have more opportunity to get to know and support their students (Fowler and Walberg, 1991; Gregory, 1992; Stockard and Mayberry, 1992).

As Wood (1992) documented in *Schools That Work,* making schools smaller is the first step toward enhancing school conditions and improving student outcomes. In 2000, based on these innovative reforms, the U. S. Congress earmarked $45 million in the Appropriations Act for the Department of Education to fund "Smaller Learning Communities" to help large high schools and school districts create subschool structures and fund strategies that make schools "feel" smaller. Congress increased the appropriation to $97 million in 2001 and in FY 2002 appropriated $142 million for the Smaller Learning Communities program.

In 2000, the U.S. Department of Education issued the first Request for Proposals (RFP) for the "Smaller Learning Communities Program" (SLC Program). According to Secretary of Education Richard W. Riley, "In smaller high schools, students can get to know their classmates and teachers better. It's these personal connections that can be so important to success in school. Size matters. We know that students thrive in smaller school settings" (Press release, October 4, 2000, USDOE, www.ed.gov/PressReleases/10-2000/100400a.html).

In the context of K–12 schools, these smaller learning communities take on a somewhat different structure and purpose from those in colleges. In the RFP, they are defined as follows:

> Structural changes for recasting large schools as a set of smaller learning communities are described in the Conference Report for the Consolidated Appropriations Act, 2000 (Pub. L. 106-113, H.R. Conference Report No. 106-479, at 1240 [1999]). Such methods include establishing small learning clusters, "houses," career academies, magnet programs, and schools-within-a-school. Structural changes are necessary but not sufficient to ensure that the reorganization will result in improved academic performance. It is also necessary to define a set of operational considerations that describe what learning looks like in the restructured smaller learning community. For example, strategies that complement a restructured large high school should include at a minimum a focus on a rigorous academic course of study. Other activities may include: freshman transition activities, advisory and adult advocate systems, academic teaming, multi-year groupings, "extra help" or accelerated learning options for students or groups of students entering below grade level, and other innovations designed to create a more personalized high school experience for students and, thus, improve student achievement [http://www.ed. gov/offices/OVAE/HS/SLCP/02apppack.doc].

Making high schools smaller is not a panacea for secondary education, but smaller, more personalized learning structures provide fertile soil in which other strategies for high school improvement may take root and succeed. Because change is easier to implement in a smaller setting, smaller learning environments create a context hospitable to reform.

Research on K–12 Learning Communities

Because of the significant investment of federal dollars in the K–12 smaller learning community initiative, significant attention has been paid to assessing the impact of small schools and smaller learning communities in public education. According to extensive research (Raywid, 1996; Williams, 1990) supported in part by federal grants over the past ten years, smaller learning communities have demonstrated that they can improve academic achievement for most students by contributing to a safer, more humane environment and a more positive overall educational experience.

With increased public concern about school safety as well as perceived and real decreases in academic performance among students, especially those in large schools, researchers have attempted to document the success of smaller learning communities. Cotton's (1996) summary of research (http://www.nwrel.org/scpd/sirs/10/c020.html) notes the positive effects of SLCs on a number of measures. Student attitudes and achievements improve, especially among minority and low socioeconomic students. There is a reduction in classroom disruptions, vandalism, truancy, and substance abuse. Students attend school more often and participate more in extracurricular activities in SLCs. The dropout rate is less than in larger schools. Interpersonal relations improve; alienation decreases. Teacher attitudes toward their work are more positive. The parallels between these findings about SLC high schools and the experiences of learning communities in the higher education community are striking.

In her summary of research on the small schools movement, Raywid (1996) notes that smaller learning communities address a number of needs and problems, including disciplinary control, school responsiveness to the needs of individual students, numbers of students participating in school activities, numbers of dropouts, and academic achievement. LaPoint and others (1996) note several advantages of smaller learning communities. They are particularly intrigued by a special type of learning community called "career academies."

Career academies are a form of smaller learning community that attracts students into tracks and integrates forms of internship, service learning, and particular constellations of content and skill courses designed to give students a jump start into a career track. According to LaPoint (1996), career academies have several advantages. They provide close, positive teacher-student relations that encourage academic achievement, better attendance, higher graduation rates, stronger adult advisory and advocacy relationships that encourage problem solving, and modifications in teachers' roles and responsibilities that foster student-teacher collaborations focused on academic goals. These career academies appear to have strong affinities to the thematic learning communities being created on campuses for undergraduates.

The federal grants supporting smaller learning communities have generated a substantial body of literature indicating that all students greatly benefit from attending small schools (see Cotton, 1996, for a recent synthesis of the literature). These studies add to the growing literature that supports the use of learning communities on college campuses to create community and a sense of smallness, particularly at large universities.

The discussion of "next steps" for learning communities is intended to expand our understanding of how learning communities function both inside and outside the academy. Clearly, different contexts create different constraints and opportunities. Whether colleges turn internally to their mission for motivation and incentives (such as a civic engagement initiatives) or externally (to the emerging partnerships with the K–12 sector), advocates for this curricular reform can find compelling evidence to support the introduction and expansion of learning communities on their campuses.

Next Steps

This chapter described how learning communities can build bridges between the university or college and its regional communities. The future sustainability and success of learning communities must be linked to agendas for higher education reform, and higher education reform is driven by both internal and external forces. Earlier chapters offered examples of how different types of institutions have experimented with restructuring time and space to enhance learning for both students and teachers. All the cases and examples described in this volume represent different contexts and points on a continuum of change.

In this chapter and throughout this book we have explored expanded visions and applications of learning communities theory. We have made connections between learning communities and research and best practices in teaching, learning, student success, faculty development, and assessment. While practitioners on college campuses work out the nuts and bolts of block scheduling and cross-campus collaborations, educational leaders can step back and see the power of a concept that restructures the learning environment. Learning communities are poised to embrace the most innovative pedagogies currently gaining widespread attention across the nation: problem-based learning; technology; and electronic portfolios that enable students to assess, document, and reflect their own learning experiences. In *Creating Learning Communities* we cautioned that the work does not end with implementation; in this book we recommend that sustaining learning communities requires a commitment to continuous improvement and support.

Higher education itself is in a state of transition—seeking to deepen and strengthen core values while expanding access and accountability. In concluding our discussion of campus-based learning communities by linking them to the challenges posed by issues in public school reform, we have attempted to shift perspective yet again. It is, after all, our students who are the measure of our success. They begin their education in the K–12 schools and must be able to move seamlessly into higher education. Educators and educational leaders, regardless of their institution or segment, all have students in common. An expanded perspective on learning communities (K–16) ties an academic curricular model to the core mission of higher education in America–developing mature citizens who are ready to live socially responsible lives and who come of age in institutions that foster best practices of a civil society.

REFERENCES

Adelman, C. *Answers in the Tool Box: Academic Intensity, Attendance Patterns, and Bachelor's Degree Attainment*. Washington, DC: U.S. Department of Education, OERI, 1999.

Alexander, R., and others. "It's Working." Presentation prepared by Iowa State University for the Academic Affairs–Student Affairs: Creating Synergy for Learning Conference. [http://web2.iastate.edu/~learncommunity/itsworking.html]. January 1999.

American Association of State Colleges and Universities (AASCU). "Stepping Forward as Stewards of Place: A Guide for Leading Public Engagement at State Colleges and Universities." [http://www.aascu.org/pdf/stewardsofplace_02.pdf]. May 2002.

American Council on Education. *To Touch the Future: Transforming the Way Teachers Are Taught*. Washington, DC. [http://www.acenet.edu/bookstore/pdf/teacher-ed-rpt.pdf]. 1999.

Anderson, J. "Developing a Learning/Teaching Style Assessment Model for Diverse Populations." In L. Suskie (ed.), *Assessment to Promote Deep Learning: Insights from AAHE's 2000 and 1999 Assessment Conferences*. Washington, DC: American Association of Higher Education, 2001.

Angelo, T. A., and Cross, K. P. *Classroom Assessment Techniques*. San Francisco: Jossey-Bass, 1993.

Association of American Colleges and Universities (AACU). *Greater Expectations: A New Vision for Learning as a Nation Goes to College*. National Panel Report. Washington, DC, 2002.

Association of American Colleges and Universities (AACU). "Press release: Association of American Colleges and Universities and Campus Compact Develop Center for Liberal Education and Civic Engagement." [http://www.aacu-edu.org/news_room/press_releases/civicengagementinstitute.cfm]. February 2003.

Astin, A. *What Matters in College.* San Francisco: Jossey-Bass, 1993.

Astin, A. W., Vogelgesang, L. J., Ikeda, E. K., and Yee, J. A. "How Service Learning Affects Students Higher Education Research Institute." [http://www.gseis.ucla.edu/slc/rhowas.html]. January 2000.

AtKisson, A. *Believing Cassandra: An Optimist Looks at a Pessimist's World.* White River Junction, VT: Chelsea Green, 1999.

Barczak, G., Smith, C., and Wilemon, D. "Managing Large-Scale Organizational Change." *Organizational Dynamics,* 1987, *16*(2), 23–35.

Barefoot, B. O. "Second National Survey of First-Year Academic Practices, 2002." Policy Center on the First Year of College. [http://www.brevard.edu/fyc/Survey2002/index.htm]. 2002.

Birnbaum, R. *How Colleges Work: The Cybernetics of Academic Organization and Leadership.* San Francisco: Jossey-Bass, 1988.

Boyer, E. *College: The Undergraduate Experience in America.* New York: Harper and Row, 1987.

Brookfield, S. D. *The Skillful Teacher.* San Francisco: Jossey-Bass, 2000.

Brookfield, S. D., and Preskill, S. *Discussion as a Way of Teaching.* San Francisco: Jossey-Bass, 1999.

Bystrom, V. "Post-Program Interviews." In Washington Center's Evaluation Committee (eds.), *Assessment in and of Collaborative Learning.* [http://www.evergreen.edu/washcenter/resources/acl/index.html]. 1995.

Cambridge, B. L. "Fostering the Scholarship of Teaching and Learning: Communities of Practice." In D. Lieberman and C. Wehlburg (eds.), *To Improve the Academy.* Bolton, MA: Anker, 2001.

Campbell, W. E., and Smith, K. A. (eds.). *New Paradigms for College Teaching.* Edina, MN: Interaction Book Company, 1997.

Canon, L. W. "Fostering Positive Race, Class and Gender Dynamics in the Classroom." *Women's Studies Quarterly,* 1990, (1/2), 126–134.

Chaffee, E. E., and Jacobson, S. W. "Creating and Changing Institutional Cultures." In M. W. Peterson, D. D. Dill, L. A. Mets, and Associates (eds.), *Planning and Management for a Changing Environment.* San Francisco: Jossey-Bass, 1997.

"The Chronicle Survey of Public Opinion on Higher Education." *Chronicle of Higher Education,* May 3, 2003, p. A11.

Cohen, M. D., and March, J. G. *Leadership and Ambiguity: The American College President.* New York: McGraw-Hill, 1974.

Colby, A., Ehrlich, T., Beaumont, E., and Stephens, J. *Educating Citizens: Preparing America's Undergraduates for Lives of Moral and Civic Responsibility.* San Francisco: Jossey-Bass, 2003.

College of Letters and Science. *Assessment of the General Education Cluster Course Experience: A Pilot Program of the College of Letters and Science.* Los Angeles: UCLA, 2001.

Collins, M. A., and Sheppard, G. "Beyond Qualitative Data: Making the Model More Meaningful." In *Curriculum Transformation: Content and Method.* Bellingham, WA: Western Washington University, Conference Proceedings for Curriculum Integration: Content and Method, 1989.

Conley, D. T. *Standards for Success: Understanding University Success.* Eugene: University of Oregon Center for Education Policy and Research, 2003.

Conway, M. A., Gardiner, J. M., Perfect, T. J., Anderson, S. J., and Cohen, G. M. "Changes in Memory Awareness During Learning: The Acquisition of Knowledge by Psychology Undergraduates." *Journal of Experimental Psychology,* 1997, *126*(4), 393–413.

Cornwell, G. H., and Stoddard, E. W. "Toward an Interdisciplinary Epistemology: Faculty Culture and Institutional Change." In B. L. Smith and J. McCann (eds.), *Reinventing Ourselves.* Bolton, MA: Anker, 2001.

Cotton, K. "School Size, School Climate, and Student Performance." Portland, OR: Northwest Regional Educational Laboratory. [http://www.nwrel.org/scpd/sirs/10/c020.html]. May 1996.

Cox, M. D. "Faculty Learning Communities: Change Agents for Transforming Institutions into Learning Organizations." In D. Lieberman and C. Wehlburg (eds.), *To Improve the Academy.* Bolton, MA: Anker, 2001.

Cross, K. P., and Steadman, M. H. *Classroom Research: Implementing the Scholarship of Teaching.* San Francisco: Jossey-Bass, 1996.

Daft, R. L. *Essentials of Organization Theory and Design.* Cincinnati, OH: South-Western College Publishing, 2001.

Dahl, R. A. "Participation and the Problem of Civic Understanding." In A. Etzioni (ed.), *Rights and the Common Good: The Communitarian Perspective.* New York: Palgrave Macmillan, 1995.

Della Piana, C. K. "Promoting Achievement for Diverse Learners: Learning Communities at the University of Texas in El Paso." Paper presented at the American Association of Higher Education National Conference, Washington, DC, March 2001.

Diamond, R. M. *Designing and Assessing Courses and Curricula.* San Francisco: Jossey-Bass, 1998.

Dunlap, L., and Stanwood, L. *Studies on the Implementation and Effectiveness of Skagit Valley College's General Education Program.* Report submitted to the General Education Committee. Mount Vernon, WA: Skagit Valley College, 1996.

Dustin, K., and Murchinson, C. "You Save Our Academic Lives." In T. Smith (ed.), *Gateways: Residential Colleges and the Freshman Year Experience.* Columbia: University of South Carolina Press, 1993.

Eaton, M., MacGregor, J., and Schoem, D. "Introduction: The Educational Promise of Service-Learning-Communities." In J. MacGregor (ed.), *Integrating Learning Communities with Service-Learning.* National Learning Communities Project Monograph Series. Olympia, WA: Evergreen State College, Washington Center for Improving the Quality of Undergraduate Education, in cooperation with the American Association for Higher Education, 2003.

Edgerton, R. "The Quality of Undergraduate Education: What's the Problem?" Pew Forum, Working Paper no. 1. Unpublished, 2003.

Ehrlich, T. *Civic Responsibility and Higher Education.* Phoenix, AZ: ACE/Oryx Press, 2000.

Entwistle, N. "Approaches to Learning and Forms of Understanding." In B. Dart and G. Boulton-Lewis (eds.), *Teaching and Learning in Higher Education.* Melbourne: Australian Council for Educational Research, 1998.

Felder, R. M., and Brent, R. "Cooperative Learning in Technical Courses: Procedures, Pitfalls, and Payoffs." [http://www.ncsu.edu/felder-public/Papers/Coopreport.html]. 1994.

Finkel, D. L. *Teaching with Your Mouth Shut*. Portsmouth, NH: Boynton/Cook Publishers, 2000.

Flateby, T. L. "The Evolution of a Participatory Approach to Assess Learning Communities at the University of South Florida." In J. MacGregor (ed.), *Doing Learning Communities Assessment: Five Campus Stories*. National Learning Communities Project Monograph Series. Olympia, WA: Evergreen State College, Washington Center for Improving the Quality of Undergraduate Education, in cooperation with the American Association for Higher Education, 2003.

Flateby, T. L., and Metzger, E. "Instructional Implications of the Cognitive Level and Quality of Writing Assessment." *Assessment Update*, 2001, *13*(1), 4–5.

Fowler, W. J., Jr., and Walberg, H. J. "School Size, Characteristics, and Outcomes." *Educational Evaluation and Policy Analysis*, 1991, *13*(2), 189–202.

Fulwiler, T. *The Journal Book*. Portsmouth, NH: Boynton/Cook, 1987.

Gabelnick, F., MacGregor, J., Matthews, R. S., and Smith, B. L. *Learning Communities: Creating Connections Among Students, Faculty, and Disciplines*. New Directions for Teaching and Learning, no. 41. San Francisco: Jossey-Bass, 1990.

Gaff, J. G. *Toward Faculty Renewal*. San Francisco: Jossey-Bass, 1975.

Goodman, P. *Compulsory Mis-Education and the Community of Scholars*. New York: Random House, 1964.

Graybeal, J. "The Team Journal." In T. Fulwiler (ed.), *The Journal Book*. Portsmouth, NH: Boynton/Cook, 1987.

Gregory, T. "Small Is Too Big: Achieving a Critical Anti-Mass in The High School." In *Source Book on School and District Size, Cost, and Quality*. Hubert H. Humphrey Institute of Public Affairs. Oak Brook, IL: North Central Regional Educational Laboratory, ED 361159, 1–31, 1992.

Guarasci, R., and Cornwell, G. *Democratic Education in an Age of Difference*. San Francisco: Jossey-Bass, 1997.

Hardiman, J. "The Evergreen State College-Tacoma Campus as a Learning Community." Paper presented at the American Association of Higher Education National Conference, Washington, DC, March 2001.

Hardiman, R., and Jackson, B. W. "Conceptual Foundations for Social Justice Courses." In M. Adams, L. A. Bell, and P. Griffin (eds.), *Teaching for Diversity and Social Justice*. New York: Routledge, 1997.

Hatch, D. "The Pilot Program: A Residential Experiment for Underclassmen." *Memo to the Faculty*. Ann Arbor: Center for Research on Learning and Teaching, University of Michigan, no. 47, 1972.

Heifetz, R. A., and Laurie, D. L. "The Work of Leadership." *Harvard Business Review*, 1997, *75*(1), 124–134.

Huba, M., and Freed, J. E. *Learner Centered Assessment on College Campuses: Shifting the Focus from Teaching to Learning*. Boston: Allyn and Bacon, 1999.

Huba, M., Epperson, D., and McFadden, M. "Final Report of the ISU Undergraduate Education Survey 2000: A Comparison of Learning Community Participants and Non-participants." Iowa State University [http://web2.iastate.edu/~learncommunity/templates/finalreport2000.pdf]. 2000.

Hurd, S. N., and Richardson, H. *Peer Facilitation Handbook*. School of Management, Syracuse University, Syracuse, NY, 2002.

Hutchings, P. "Promoting a Culture of Teaching and Learning." In D. DeZure (ed.), *Learning from Change*. Sterling, VA: Stylus, 2000.

Ibarra, R. *Beyond Affirmative Action: Reframing the Context of Higher Education.* Madison: University of Wisconsin Press, 2001.

IUPUI Template for First Year Seminars. [http://www.universitycollege.iupui.edu/]. May 2002.

Jacobs, F. H. "The Five-Tiered Approach to Evaluation: Context and Implementation." In H. B. Weiss and F. H. Jacobs, (eds.), *Evaluating Family Programs.* New York: Aldine De Gruyter, 1988.

Johnson, D. W., and Johnson, R. T. *Learning Together and Alone.* Boston: Allyn and Bacon, 1999.

Jones, G. R. *Organizational Theory: Text and Cases.* Upper Saddle River, NJ: Prentice-Hall, 2001.

Jones, P., Morris, N., Levine, J., and Foley, B. "Developing an Empirically Based Typology of Attitudes Towards Participation in Learning Community Courses." Paper Presented at the American Association of Higher Education Assessment Conference, Boston, June 2002. [Available on-line at http://www.temple.edu/lc/reports.html].

Kezar, A., Hirsch, D. J., and Burack, C. *Understanding the Role of Academic and Student Affairs Collaboration in Creating a Successful Learning Environment.* New Directions for Higher Education, no. 116. San Francisco: Jossey-Bass, 2001.

Kido, J., Parson, W., and Decker, E. "Team Planning for Diversity in Learning Community Programs." Workshop presented at the Evergreen State College General Education Institute, Olympia, WA, June 2000.

Kitano, M. K. "What a Course Will Look Like After Multicultural Change." In A. Morey, and M. K. Kitano (eds.), *Multicultural Course Transformation in Higher Education: A Broader Truth.* Needham Heights, MA: Allyn and Bacon, 1997.

Klein, T. "From Classroom to Learning Community: One Professor's Reflections." *About Campus,* 2000, July/August, *5*(3), 12–19.

Klonsky, M. *Small Schools: The Numbers Tell a Story. A Review of the Research and Current Experiences.* Chicago: The Small Schools Workshop. ERIC Document Reproduction Service no. ED386517, 1995.

Kuh, G. "Guiding Principles for Creating Seamless Learning Environments for Undergraduates." *Journal of College Student Development,* 1996, *37*(2), 135–148.

Kurotsuchi Inkelas, K. *A Tide on Which All Boats Ride: The Effects of Living-Learning Program Participation on Undergraduate Outcomes at the University of Michigan.* Ann Arbor: Division of Student Affairs, University of Michigan, 1999.

LaPoint, V., Jordan, W., McPartland, J. M., and Penn Towns, D. *The Talent Development High School: Essential Components.* (Report no. 1). Baltimore, MD: Johns Hopkins University/Howard University, Center for Research on the Education of Students Placed at Risk, 1996.

Levine Laufgraben, J. "The Assessment Journey of the Learning Communities at Temple University: Learning to Assess and Assessing to Learn." In J. MacGregor (ed.), *Doing Learning Communities Assessment: Five Campus Stories.* National Learning Communities Project Monograph Series. Olympia, WA: Evergreen State College, Washington Center for Improving the Quality of Undergraduate Education, in cooperation with the American Association for Higher Education, 2003.

Levine Laufgraben, J. "Learning Communities." In M. L. Upcraft, J. N. Gardner, and B. O. Barefoot (eds.), *Challenging and Supporting the First-Year Student: A Handbook for Improving the First Year of College.* San Francisco: Jossey-Bass, 2004.

Lieberman, D. A., and Guskin, A. E. "The Essential Role of Faculty Development in New Higher Education Models." In C. Wehlburg and S. Chadwick-Blossey (eds.), *To Improve the Academy.* Bolton, MA: Anker, 2003.

Light, R. J. *Making the Most of College.* Cambridge, MA: Harvard University Press, 2001.

Lowell, N. *Freshman Interest Groups, Autumn 1996: Faculty Survey.* Research Notes N-97-2. Seattle: Office of Educational Assessment, University of Washington, 1997.

MacGregor, J. "Goals and Practices Associated with Learning Community Programs." [http://learningcommons.evergreen.edu/03_start_entry.asp#23]. 1996.

MacGregor, J. "Teaching Communities Within Learning Communities." [http://learningcommons.evergreen.edu/pdf/spring2000b.pdf]. Spring 2000.

MacGregor, J., Smith, B. L., Matthews, R., and Gabelnick, F. "Learning Community Models." [http://learningcommons.evergreen.edu/docs/LCmodels.ppt]. May 2002.

Mager, R. F. *Preparing Instructional Objectives.* Belmont, CA: Fearon, 1975.

Mallory, B., and Thomas, N. "Promoting Ethical Action Through Democratic Dialogue." *Change,* 2003, *35*(5), Sept./Oct., 10–17.

Malnarich, G. "Introduction." *Critical Moments Newsletter,* no. 1. Olympia, WA: Washington Center for Improving the Quality of Undergraduate Education, 2002.

Marchese, T. J. "The New Conversations About Learning: Insights from Neuroscience and Anthropology, Cognitive Science and Work-Place Studies." In B. Cambridge (ed.), *Assessing Impact: Evidence and Action.* Washington, DC: American Association for Higher Education, 1997.

Marton, F. "Toward a Theory of Quality in Higher Education." In B. Dart and G. Boulton-Lewis (eds.), *Teaching and Learning in Higher Education.* Melbourne: Australian Council for Educational Research, 1998.

McGrath, E., and others. "Welcome, Freshman!" *Time,* September 10, 2001, *158*(10), 64–77.

McKeachie, W. J. *McKeachie's Teaching Tips: Strategies, Research, and Theory for College and University Teachers* (11th ed.). New York: Houghton Mifflin, 2002.

Meiklejohn, A. *The Experimental College.* New York: HarperCollins, 1932.

Merriam, S. B., and others. *Qualitative Research in Practice.* San Francisco: Jossey-Bass, 2002.

Meyers, C., and Jones, T. B. *Promoting Active Learning: Strategies for the College Classroom.* San Francisco: Jossey-Bass, 1993.

Middle States Commission on Higher Education. *Student Learning Assessment: Options and Resources.* Philadelphia, 2003.

Millis, B. J., and Cottell, P. G., Jr. *Cooperative Learning for Higher Education Faculty.* Westport, CT: American Council on Education, 1998.

Montecino, G., Smith, L., and Young, J. *Information Technology: Learning and Assessment.* Fairfax, VA: New Century College First-Year Program, George Mason University, 2000.

Morey, A. I. "Organizational Change and Implementation Strategies for Multicultural Infusion." In A. Morey and M. K. Kitano (eds.), *Multicultural Course Transformation in Higher Education: A Broader Truth.* Needham Heights, MA: Allyn and Bacon, 1997.

Morey, A. I., and Kitano, M. K. (eds.). *Multicultural Course Transformation in Higher Education: A Broader Truth.* Needham Heights, MA: Allyn and Bacon, 1997.

Moses, R., and Cobb, C. C. *Radical Equations: Civil Rights from Mississippi to the Algebra Project.* Boston: Beacon Press, 2001.

National Center for Education Statistics. *Digest of Statistics.* [http://nces.ed.gov/pubs2003/digest02/ch_3.asp#1]. 2003.

National Commission on Civic Renewal. *A Nation of Spectators: How Civic Disengagement Weakens America and What We Can Do About It.* College Park: University of Maryland, 1998.

National Institute of Education. *Involvement in Learning: Realizing the Potential of American Higher Education.* Study Group on the Conditions of Excellence in American Education. Washington, DC: NIE, Department of Education, 1984.

Nelson, A. *Education and Democracy: The Meaning of Alexander Meiklejohn, 1872–1964.* Madison: University of Wisconsin, 2001.

Newmann, F., and Oliver, D. "Education and Community." *Harvard Education Review,* 1967, *37*(1), 61–106.

Oates, K. "New Century College: Connecting the Classroom to the World." In *Learning Communities in Research Universities.* National Learning Communities Project Monograph Series. Olympia, WA: Evergreen State College, Washington Center for Improving the Quality of Undergraduate Education, in cooperation with the American Association for Higher Education, 2003.

Palmer, P. J. *The Courage to Teach.* San Francisco: Jossey-Bass, 1998.

Parks Daloz, L., Keen, C., Keen, J., and Daloz Parks, S. *Common Fire: Leading Lives of Commitment in a Complex World.* Boston: Beacon Press, 1996.

Patton, M. Q. *Utilization-Focused Evaluation.* Thousand Oaks, CA: Sage, 1997.

Peterson, M. W., Dill, D. D., Mets, L. A., and Associates. *Planning and Management for a Changing Environment.* San Francisco: Jossey-Bass, 1997.

Rasmussen, G., and Skinner, E. "Learning Communities: Getting Started." [http://www.mcli.dist.maricopa.edu/ilc/monograph/index.html]. 2001.

Raywid, M. A. *Downsizing Schools in Big Cities.* ERIC Digest. no. 112, ED393958, 1996.

Rendon, L. A., and Hope, R. O. "An Educational System in Crisis." In L. Rendon and R. Hope (eds.), *Educating a New Majority: Transforming America's Educational System for Diversity.* San Francisco: Jossey-Bass, 1996.

Rong, Y. "A Literature Review of the History and Perspectives of College Student Classroom and Residence Hall Learning." *Journal of College and University Student Housing,* 1998, *27*(2), 3–8.

Ryan, M. "Residential Colleges: A Legacy of Living and Learning Together." *Change,* Sept./Oct. 1992, *24*(5), 26–35.

Ryan, M. *A Collegiate Way of Living: Residential Colleges and a Yale Education.* New Haven, CT: John Edwards College, Yale University, 2001.

Schneider, C. G. "Preparing Students for What? School-College Alignment in an Era of Greater Expectations." *Peer Review,* 2003, *5*(2).

Schneider, C. G., and Shoenberg, R. "Habits Hard to Break." *Change,* 1999, *31*(2), 30–35.

Schoem, D. "Making a Difference." *Peer Review,* 2001, *3/4*(4/1), 38–41.

Schoem, D. "Transforming Undergraduate Education: Moving Beyond Distinct Undergraduate Initiatives." *Change Magazine,* 2002, Nov./Dec., *34*(6).

Schoem, D., and Hurtado, S. (eds.). *Intergroup Dialogue: Deliberative Democracy in School, College, Community and Workplace.* Ann Arbor: University of Michigan Press, 2001.

Schoem, D., and Pasque, P. "Learning for the Common Good: A Diverse Community Lives and Learns Together in the Michigan Community Scholars Program." In J. MacGregor (ed.), *Integrating Learning Communities with Service Learning.* National Learning Communities Project Monograph Series, Olympia, WA: Evergreen State College, the Washington Center for Improving the Quality of Undergraduate Eduacation, in cooperation with the American Association for Higher Education, 2003.

Schön, D. A. *The Reflective Practitioner*. New York: Basic Books, 1983.

Schroeder, C., and Hurst, J. "Designing Learning Environments That Integrate Curricular and Cocurricular Experiences." *Journal of College Student Development,* 1996, *37*(2), March/April, 174–180.

Schroeder, C., Minor, F., and Tarkow, T. "Learning Communities: Partnerships Between Academic and Student Affairs." In J. H. Levine (ed.), *Learning Communities: New Structures, New Partnerships for Learning*. Monograph 26. Columbia: University of South Carolina, National Resource Center for the First-Year Experience and Students in Transition, 1999.

Shapiro, N. S. "University of Maryland College Park Scholars: Creating a Coherent Lens for General Education." In J. O'Connor and Associates (eds.), *Learning Communities in Research Universities*. National Learning Communities Project Monograph Series. Olympia, WA: Evergreen State College, Washington Center for Improving the Quality of Undergraduate Education, in cooperation with the American Association for Higher Education, 2003.

Shapiro, N. S., and Levine, J. H. *Creating Learning Communities: A Practical Guide to Winning Support, Organizing for Change, and Implementing Programs*. San Francisco: Jossey-Bass, 1999.

Silverman, S. L., and Casazza, M. E. *Learning and Development: Making Connections to Enhance Teaching*. San Francisco: Jossey-Bass, 1999.

Sizer, T. *Horace's Compromise: The Dilemma of the American High School*. Boston: Houghton Mifflin, 1984.

Skinner, R., and Chapman, C. "Service-Learning and Community Service in K-12 Public Schools." NCES no. 1999043. [http://nces.ed.gov/pubsearch/pubsinfo.asp?pubid=1999043]. 1999.

Smith, B. L. "The Challenges of Learning Communities as a Growing National Movement." *Peer Review,* 2001, *3/4*(4/1), 4–8.

Smith. B. L., and McCann, J. (eds.). *Reinventing Ourselves: Interdisciplinary Education, Collaborative Learning, and Experimentation in Higher Education*. Bolton, MA: Anker, 2001.

Smith, T. (ed.). *First Annual International Conference of Residential Colleges and Living/Learning Centers Proceedings*. Kirksville: Northeast Missouri State University, 1992.

Stanwood, L., and Dunlap, L. "The Assessment Chase: The Changing Shape of Assessment in Shaping Change at Skagit Valley College." In J. MacGregor (ed.), *Doing Learning Communities Assessment: Five Campus Stories*. National Learning Communities Project Monograph Series. Olympia, WA: Evergreen State College, Washington Center for Improving the Quality of Undergraduate Education, in cooperation with the American Association for Higher Education, 2003.

Stein, R. F., and Hurd, S. N. *Using Student Teams in the Classroom*. Bolton, MA: Anker, 2000.

Stockard, J., and Mayberry, M. "Resources and School and Classroom Size." In J. Stockard and M. Mayberry (eds.), *Effective Educational Environments*. Newbury Park, CA: Corwin Press, 1992.

Suskie, L. Handouts from workshop presented at Temple University. [http://www.temple.edu/lc/suskie_handouts.pdf]. June 2003.

Swing, R. L. "Benchmarking First-Year Seminars: A National Study of Learning Outcomes." [http://www.brevard.edu/fyc/randy/FYI2002.htm]. June 2002.

Tierney, W. G. "Overcoming Obstacles to Reform." *About Campus,* 2001, *6*(2), 20–24.

Tinto, V. *Leaving College: Rethinking the Causes and Cures of Student Attrition.* Chicago: University of Chicago Press, 1987.

Treisman, U. "Studying Students Studying Calculus: A Look at the Lives of Minority Mathematics Students in College." *College Mathematics Journal,* 1992, *23*(5), 362–372.

Trow, K. B. *Habits of Mind: The Experimental College Program at Berkeley.* Berkeley: Institute of Governmental Studies Press, University of California, 1998.

Tussman, J. *Experiment at Berkeley.* New York: Oxford University Press, 1969.

U.S. Department of Education. *A Nation at Risk.* National Commission on Excellence in Education. Washington, DC: U.S. Department of Education, 1983.

U.S. Department of Education. "Smaller Learning Communities Program Application for Grants." [http://www.ed.gov/offices/OVAE/HS/SLCP/02apppack.doc]. 2003.

Vaill, P. B. *Learning as a Way of Being: Strategies for Survival in a World of Permanent White Water.* San Francisco: Jossey-Bass, 1996.

van Slyck, P., and Koolsbergen, W. "Thirty Students, Twenty-five Nationalities: Diversity and Learning Communities at LaGuardia Community College." Paper presented at the American Association of Higher Education National Conference, Washington, DC, March 2001.

Vavrus, M. *Transforming the Multicultural Education of Teachers: Theory, Research and Practice.* New York: Teachers College Press, 2002.

Venezia, A., Kirst, M. W., and Antonio, A. L. *Betraying the College Dream: How Disconnected K-12 and Postsecondary Education Systems Undermine Student Aspirations.* Stanford, CA: The Bridge Project, 2003.

Waltzer, K. "Mad About Madison." *MSU Alumni Magazine,* Fall 1992.

Weimer, M. *Learner-Centered Teaching.* San Francisco: Jossey-Bass, 2002.

White, K. "Mid-Course Adjustments: Using Small Group Instructional Diagnoses to Improve Teaching and Learning." In Washington Center's Evaluation Committee (eds.), *Assessment in and of Collaborative Learning.* [http://www.evergreen.edu/washcenter/resources/acl/index.c4html]. 1995.

Wiggins, G., and McTighe, J. *Understanding by Design.* Alexandria, VA: Association for Supervision and Curriculum Development, 1998.

Williams, D. T. *The Dimensions of Education: Recent Research on School Size.* Working Papers Series, Strom Thurmond Institute of Government and Public Affairs. Clemson, SC: Clemson University. (ED 347006), December 1990.

Wood, G. H. *Schools That Work: America's Most Innovative Public Education Programs.* New York: Dutton, 1992.

Wright, B. D. "Assessing Student Learning." In D. DeZure (ed.), *Learning from Change.* Sterling, VA: Stylus, 2000.

Wunsch, E. "The Pilot Program—An Attack on Impersonality and Academic Isolation in a Large College." *Memo to the Faculty,* no. 20. Ann Arbor, MI: Center for Research on Learning and Teaching, 1966.

Index